THE ABCs OF MAKING MONEY 4 Teens

3 Easy Steps to Freedom

Dr. Denis L. Cauvier & Alan Lysaght

Wealth Solutions Press

Published in 2005 by
Wealth Solutions Press Inc.
Media inquiries **only:** 1-866-218-8932.

First Printing by
Wealth Solutions Press Inc. in April 2005
Design and Production by Donna Harris Design, http://www3.sympatico.ca/donnaharris0

Printed in Canada

Library and Archives Canada Cataloguing in Publication

Cauvier, Denis L., 1963-
    The ABCs of making money 4 teens : 3 easy steps to
freedom / Denis L. Cauvier, Alan Lysaght
Lysaght, Alan, 1962-

ISBN 0-9733549-3-3

    1. Finance, Personal. 2. Money. 3. Teenagers--Finance,
Personal. I. Lysaght, Alan II. Title. III. Title: ABCs of making
money 4 teens.

HG179.C334 2005   332'.02400835   C2005-901942-5

This publication is designed to provide knowledgeable and dependable information regarding the subject matter covered. However, it is sold with the understanding that the authors and publisher are not engaged in rendering legal, financial, or other professional advice. Laws and practices vary from country to country and state to state and if legal or other expert assistance is required, the services of a professional should be sought. The authors and the publisher specifically disclaim any liability that is incurred from the use or application of the contents of this book.

Introduction

As consultants we have spent years researching and working with teen groups, teachers, youth and guidance counsellors. Over the years teens like you have shared your experiences with us and from you we have learned a lot about the challenges you face every day.

SOME of these CHALLENGES can lead you to feel:

- ☞ **Lost and out of control**
- ☞ **Overpowered by peer pressures**
- ☞ **Limited by lack of money**
- ☞ **Overwhelmed with school, family and social activities**
- ☞ **Moody and depressed**
- ☞ **Frustrated with health and body image issues**
- ☞ **Nagged by family members**
- ☞ **Pressure to perform at school or in sports**
- ☞ **Pressure from relationships**
- ☞ **Stressed and uncertain about the future**
- ☞ **A lack of personal freedom**

CONSIDERING HOW IMPORTANT money is to our lives it's amazing how little time we spend learning about it. If money was a pop idol or a basketball star, you'd know all about it. Having money is cool, so why isn't knowing all about it cool as well? Probably because we think of it as too boring or too complicated to bother learning about. Well, we're here to share with you that you can easily learn **how money works**, how **it can work for you**, and that you can **have fun doing it**. We all know how to ride bikes, work a computer

Having money is COOL

FREEDOM IS BASICALLY about choice. The more choices you have, the freer you are. The purpose of this book is first and foremost to help you make money. But while having more **money** means **more choices**, we do not believe it will necessarily solve all your problems. That's why the ABCs go beyond money. The systematic approach we take to getting and keeping money— The ABCs—will solve problems

and improve your wellbeing in every aspect of your life. Pull your life together in this one crucial area, your net worth, and the lessons you learn will help you put everything else together as well.

REMEMBER AS YOU go through this book, to ask yourself constantly how the principles covered in each section relate to the non-money issues that are important to you.

and some even know how to speak a second language. Many of these skills are tough to learn.

3

The funny thing is that learning the basics of making money is even easier.

NOT HAVING A proper understanding of money limits your choices. It prevents you from having the things you want, forces you to work long hours doing jobs you don't enjoy, and can wreck families and marriages. Yet, we learn very little about money in schools, in colleges or on the job. That lack of knowledge makes us more easily exploited and even ripped off by people less honest than ourselves. So, what we're going to do in this book is to walk you through some of the simple and fun strategies to make and keep money.

WE'VE BEEN TRAVELING around the world for many years helping companies and individuals improve their finances. We've worked with lots of self-made millionaires and even a few billionaires, and over the years certain themes and lessons keep reappearing. They are consistent, they are not rocket science and they're universal:

Anyone **Can Be** RICH!

THERE ARE LOADS of self-made millionaires, and they're just like you and me. They made wise choices, avoided many wealth limiting Behaviors and, more than anything else, they believed in themselves. We're going to share some of these secrets with you so that you too can be financially successful.

IN THIS BOOK you'll learn simple strategies that will save you lots of money, and we'll share some

stories of teens just like you who have made thousands of dollars—even millions—while doing nothing more than playing at and developing their hobbies. The process was not painful for them, and it won't be for you. It's simple and fun to play.

LET'S SAY IT another way: we do not believe that the object of life is simply to make money. We are saying that money gives you choices. Your choice may be to travel around the world, get more electronic toys, buy a fast car, or you may want to set up a mission for the under-privileged at home or in a third world country. It's your choice. Our job is to give you the knowledge that lets you make your own choices. Choice is freedom.

THIS BOOK HAS three chapters. The first deals with Attitudes and, as you've probably heard before, they are critical to success. If you understand this section and apply the principles, then everything that follows will become clearer, faster. If at this moment you have it in your head that success, in school or sports, socially or financially, is something that happens only to other people, guess what: you will be proven **right**. Nothing happens without **Winning Attitudes**. Whether you want to win for your team, to build a empire or simply to live life more comfortably,

overcoming any negative Attitudes and believing in yourself are the first critical steps.

THE SECOND CHAPTER deals with the "how to's" of money. Here we'll show you simple, fun ways to save and, most importantly, to avoid being ripped off when buying and saving. The chapter explores the two bottom-line principles of money management (a) being practical, and (b) having fun while saving. Over time these will allow you to live comfortably and get the things you want.

> **Make your own choices. CHOICE is freedom.**

THE THIRD CHAPTER takes it all a step further: It's about Creating wealth and it's more aggressive that the first two chapters. See it as the difference between dial-up Internet and high speed. They'll both get you the information, but the quicker way requires a little more effort and creativity. Section 3 is not for everybody, yet, as you'll see from the many stories we've collected, anyone can do it! We learn year after year that most people have advantages and abilities they're not fully using. So, what we're going to show you is that by doing what you already like to do, and combining that with the assets available to you or easily obtained from someone else, you can make a lot of money doing what you love.

You'll **learn** many things in this process but two of the most **important** are:

1 How to use the money you already have more efficiently.
2 How to make a lot of money while having fun.

WE DON'T COVER "get rich quick" schemes or anything illegal. We don't need to. Everything we talk about involves discovering the potential and blessings that every single person was born with and using them to your advantage. Nobody who pays attention and participates will be left behind because we believe that everybody is a winner in some unique way. This book is dedicated to helping each and every one of you discover what that means for you.

WE DECIDED TO write this book following the international success of "The ABCs of Making Money" which was released in 2003. We started hearing **loads** of **inspiring stories** from people who had taken charge of their lives and who had started their own businesses. Some of the most consistently innovative ideas came from teenagers who had lit-

tle or no experience in business. It was awesome to discover how many of these successful businesses were not just about making money but involved recycling, saving the planet in some way, and giving back to the community. We were inspired. Meeting these remarkable people reminded us that we all have a lot to learn. A crucial lesson: age is not a factor. You are never too old, or in your case, too young to learn something new.

WHEN WE TALK to teens they tell us they want the freedom to get what they want without begging their parents for the money, and also that making money should be fun. In short, Money = Freedom. Some have been told that because they're kids they are not smart enough to understand money issues.

WE BELIEVE
teens have the power to achieve their dreams and that they can accomplish what they set out to do.

WE BELIEVE
you're never too young to understand how to make your own money.

WE BELIEVE
that business is not the exclusive domain of adults.

WE BELIEVE
that teens, as a consumer group, have awesome buying power and deserve more respect from businesses and advertisers.

WE BELIEVE
that teens, like any group, gain power when they accept responsibility for their own destiny.

AS YOU'LL SEE from the many stories we'll share throughout this book, teenagers have accomplished amazing things using only available resources and, most importantly, their imaginations. To help and support those who are just starting out we dedicate this book to you and hope to hear about your success stories real soon. You can even email them to us at INFO@ABCS4TEENS.COM. We are also pledging a portion of the retail sales from this book to several teen charities.

Good Luck
ENJOY!

Happiness
Ensurity

Attitudes for Making Money

Are you ready to make more money? It's not as silly a question as it might sound. We've found that the simple desire to be financially independent or successful in any activity, whether in school, sports, socially or financially, is only the first step along the path. The first hurdle is to match that desire with the right Attitudes. Once these are in line then you can learn the specific skills and get into action. But the Attitude has to be there—if you suspect deep down you will not be able to make money or achieve any other personal goal, then you won't. As simple as this truth is, it is the hardest to see and act upon. For this reason we begin the book by examining Attitudes—the way we think—and how to change forever those Attitudes that stand between you and success.

LET'S TALK A bit about the word Attitude. It has some bad meanings, and some of those meanings can cost you money. We'd like to offer a different take on the word, because your current definition may be holding you back from success.

When the word is misused, it has a NASTY tone to it, such as:

"Change your Attitude!"

"You've got a real Attitude problem."

"You've got SOME Attitude."

SO LET'S BE clear: When you see the word "Attitude" in this book, it is not a 'put-down' or negative judgment on anyone! Attitude—the right Attitude—is good. Your Attitude is who you are. It's your dominant thoughts and beliefs that create your reality. We're not making any judgments on anyone's Attitudes; what we're saying is that if you have a negative Attitude about something—and in this case we mean Attitudes about money—that will negatively affect everything else in your life. So, if you want to be rich, for example, you have a much better chance of getting there if your Attitude is positive rather than negative.

IF YOU FOLLOW all the money-saving or money-generating strategies in Chapter B (Behaviors) and C (Creations) of this book you

It's your dominant thoughts and beliefs that create your reality

will be well on your way to achieving your money-making goals. By taking some time to look at and, if you think it's necessary, modifying your Attitudes, you will

become much more successful. The easiest way to approach this is to ask yourself a simple question: Are you happy with everything you have? If your answer is "Yes" that's great and you're ready to move on to the next steps. If the answer is "No" then we want to share with you how you can achieve your goals quicker. It's as if you want to go from New York to Los Angeles. You could walk there, you could use your skateboard, a bicycle, a car or a plane. Each method will eventually get you there. The fastest way is the airplane. A positive Attitude towards money is similar. You'll get to your destination quicker and easier if you think that way. Identifying, and then sorting out any challenges in this area will make the rest of the strategies much easier to achieve and much more successful.

WHEN YOU THINK about the words wealth and money what thoughts immediately come into your mind? Are all these thoughts positive?

Some of your thoughts concerning wealth and money may not all be positive. Have you ever heard these Attitudes about wealth and money?

- **Money does not grow on trees.**
- **Money cannot buy happiness.**
- **You have to pay your dues.**
- **Wealthy people are unhappy.**
- **Wealth corrupts.**
- **It takes lots of money to make money.**
- **Wealthy people never enjoy happy relationships.**
- **You have to be born into money.**

"Sooner or later, those who win are those who think they can."

— Richard Bach, Author of Jonathan Livingston Seagull

HOW MANY OF these beliefs are negative? Here's another way to look at it. The wooden baseball bat you use was once a tree; your favorite magazine as well as the books you use to learn about the world are all printed on paper, which came from trees. Tony Hawk has made a fortune in part from his boarding magazines.

In the space provided below take the time to **write** down the first five **beliefs** surrounding money and wealth that come into your head.

1 Success
2 Happiness
3 Ensurity
4 Power
5 Wellness

8

Acoustic guitars and several other musical instruments all come from wood. So, in fact, money does grow on trees. The point is that it's all in the way you look at things.

AS WE TRAVEL the world we constantly hear these myths repeated. If you've heard—**and accept**—even one of these beliefs, it will hold you back from making money. By the end of this chapter we hope to prove this important principle to you, and show you that having a positive Attitude will have a major impact on your financial future. Please don't misunderstand—if you just think happy money thoughts alone, a large bag of cash will NOT magically materialize. Life doesn't work that way. Having positive money-making Attitudes is only the beginning. You will also need to engage in the correct money-making Behaviors we'll reveal in the next chapter. But please, resist the natural temptation to jump ahead to the next chapter and start reading about money-making Behaviors. That's because the starting point for making money is a **rock-solid foundation** of positive Attitudes about yourself. Only then can you use those positive thoughts to direct your daily Behaviors.

NOW IS THE perfect point to pause for a moment. It's time to come up with your own personal definition of wealth.

A DICTIONARY DEFINES wealth as: "The state of being rich; great abundance of anything." That may mean money or it could mean being healthy and surrounded by loved ones. Write your own definition in the space provided above.

MY Definition of WEALTH

Having a self-satisfied amount of money and thus, a more successful life.

DENIS & ALAN'S DEFINITION OF WEALTH:

Having what you WANT, and WANTING what you have.

NOW THAT YOU'VE created a definition of wealth you are more likely to achieve it than those who do not have one. This brings up the question: Why are some people more financially successful than others?

WE'VE found that successful people have a lot in COMMON with each other:

1 They know what they want out of life.

2 They stay positive and believe in their ability to win even in tough times.

3 They're willing to invest the time and energy it takes to succeed.

4 They set meaningful and challenging goals for themselves.

5 They have a Success game plan to achieve their goals and they work towards those goals every single day.

RYAN HRELJAC

SO, WHAT DOES all this mean? Here's an incredible example of someone whose selfless personal crusade has saved thousands of lives.

WATER COVERS ALMOST 75% of the earth's surface. Most of us take it for granted; yet it's absolutely essential for life. Tragically, more than one billion people do not have access to clean drinking water.

IN JANUARY 1998, six year old **Ryan Hreljac** listened as his first grade teacher, Nancy Prest, told the class about the thousands of children dying from polluted, disease-infested water in Africa. Ryan ran home and immediately committed himself to raising money to help change that terrible situation. "I thought the whole world lived like we did. I thought that all kids grew up with nice houses and played with toys and went to school. When I heard that wasn't true I was shocked and needed to help change things. I couldn't stand the fact that children were dying because they couldn't get clean water."

HIS PARENTS, SUSAN and Mark, agreed to let him earn the money by doing extra jobs around the house. So, while his brothers and friends played outside Ryan put in the hours doing odd jobs, earning money a dollar or two at a time. Four months later he had managed to raise $70. which is what he thought was the cost of a clean water well. When he approached WaterCan, a charity dedicated to helping poorer countries access clean water, he told them about an extra $5 he had included "To buy some hot lunches for the people digging the well." WaterCan told him "$70 would indeed buy a hand pump that needs to be put on top of a well, but digging a well costs $2,000!"

NOT VERY APPETIZING

THE HUGE DIFFERENCE between what he had and what he needed would have made most people give up. Not Ryan. He was committed to saving children in Africa. "I thought, well, I'd just have to do a few more chores. It won't take that long. I want everyone in Africa to have clean water." Ryan was **relentless** about getting people in his family, his school and his community involved. In one Hike-A-Thon alone they raised $4,500. By

September, Ryan and friends had raised the necessary money and workers started drilling a well beside Angolo Primary School in northern Uganda. Prior to that the closest water came from a swamp over 3 miles away. Typhoid, infestations of intestinal worms and other deadly diseases carried in the unclean water killed one of every five children in the community.

DIGGING A WELL by hand is very slow, difficult work. Having a drilling machine would make a huge difference in the number of wells that could be finished but they cost $25,000. When he heard this, Ryan, in his quiet, unassuming way simply said "I'll raise the money for that."

IN SEPTEMBER 1998, a newspaper ran a story about Ryan. Other papers across the country picked up the story, as did many TV stations. "At one point I had to stop doing so many chores because I was doing interviews and speeches all the time. I was also busy writing organizations for donations for the drill and then writing back 'Thank you' letters. It just started to grow and grow." And so did the contributions from across the country. In addition to raising money, Ryan's next-door neighbors decided to donate their frequent flyer miles to help Ryan and his family go and see the people he was helping. In July 2000, Ryan and his parents made the long trip to Uganda. As they drove down the dusty, bumpy road towards Angolo Primary School, children started shouting Ryan's name. To his shock their guide told him that everyone for hundreds of miles around knew his name! Then they arrived at the school where 5,000 children from the area, all cheering for Ryan, greeted them. "It was great to be there and to see the look on their faces. They were really happy to finally have clean water. I'll never forget the look on their faces. It was very satisfying."

Photo courtesy of Ryan's Well Foundation

He raised $70...he THOUGHT that was the cost of a CLEAN water well.

SINCE CONSTRUCTION OF the first well Ryan and students around the world have continued their fund raising activities. Their efforts have inspired many other schools to raise money for new wells in Africa as well as other countries. Countless other people have contributed to this project after hearing Ryan's story. "I think we've made a dif-ference, but we haven't done it alone. We've had great support from everyone."

IN 2001 RYAN set up the Ryan's Well Foundation (www.ryan-swell.org). To date, after 7 years of painstaking work, Ryan has helped to raise over $1,000,000 and completed 155 clean-water wells and sanitation projects for the grateful nations of Uganda, Zimbabwe, Kenya, Malawi, Ethi-opia, Tanzania, Guyana, Guate-mala and Nigeria, bringing clean water to more than 250,000 people.

"IF YOU HAVE a goal and try really hard, you can do anything you want. There really are no lim-its." Seemingly there are no lim-its to Ryan's passion for helping other people. "I want to be a water engineer when I grow up. I want to work until all of Africa has clean water."

EVERY DAY 6,000 children die from drinking contaminated water. We salute Ryan and the desperately needed work he started. Please check out his website to learn more: HTTP://WWW.RYANSWELL.ORG

WE'VE had GREAT **support**

"Do everything possible on your part to live in peace with everybody."
— Romans 12:18

My Big Picture

How about you? Do you have anything that you're passionate about? Here are some questions to consider.

What are you passionate about?

_____

_____

_____

If you were financially independent how would you spend your time?

_____

_____

_____

What would people say is your greatest strength?

_____

_____

_____

Who in history do you admire most, and why?

_____

_____

_____

If you could solve a social problem or injustice, what would it be?

_____

_____

_____

How would the ability to make money affect your chances of dealing with any of the above issues?

_____

_____

_____

NOW THAT YOU have your definition of wealth and you have considered the above questions, the next step is to write down what success means to you. Success is

> **A generous person will be in a better position TO HELP PEOPLE.**

often a combination of wealth and personal goals. Remember that the acquisition of wealth isn't the goal; it's a tool to a wide variety of goals. Money is like an amplifier.

> **"What is your life?"**
> — James 4:14

When someone sings into a microphone it doesn't make them better or worse it just makes their abilities clearer to more people. It's the same with money. A mean or self-centered person will likely remain the same even though

> **"There is nothing wrong when men possess riches but the wrong comes when riches possess men."**
> — Rev. Billy Graham

their bank account is enriched. On the other hand a generous, considerate person who attains wealth will simply be in a better position to help other people.

WE BELIEVE THAT success means being happy with your life, both as it is now and where it's headed. By clearly defining what success means to you personally—whether it is having a million dollars in the bank, being able to travel to cool places, owning a

> **"Your direction is more important than your speed."**
> — Richard L. Evans

dream car, having more time for your family and friends or giving more of your time and effort to a favorite cause—you have created a target. If you have not taken the time to define your target, opportunities will be lost because you are not focused enough to recognize them when they appear.

IF THE FIRST part of achieving success is a winning attitude then the second part is knowing where to focus your effort. In other words, your goals. Imagine for a moment an Olympic medalist in archery who is asked to hit a target for a million-dollar prize. That person knows all the technical steps and expects to win. Just before shooting, however, a hood is placed over the archer's head, who is then spun around three times. What do you think would happen? The archer would be lucky to come anywhere close to the target. Why? Because **You can't HIT a target you can't SEE!**

THE SAME PRINCIPLE is at work in getting what you want out of life. You may have the knowledge,

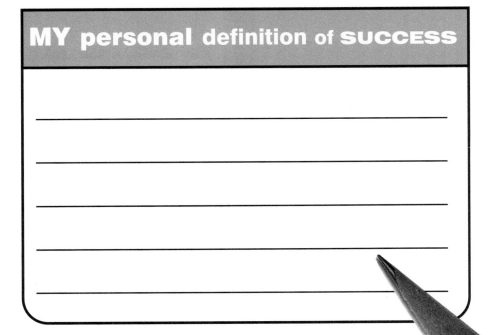

MY personal definition of SUCCESS

the skills, supportive friends and family, and you may read this book from cover to cover, but unless you can see your target you will remain unfocused and disoriented, and you will never really enjoy true success.

NOW THAT YOU have defined what wealth means to you, and you have a definition for success, you have effectively taken off your "blindfold" and have a target in sight. One of the things you may discover as a result of this exercise is that you have a more realistic understanding of what is needed to achieve your goals.

IF GOALS ARE so important, why do so few people set them? Here are the most common reasons:

- People don't understand that setting goals helps them get what they want out of life.
- People often don't know how to set goals. It's not a skill that is normally taught in schools or at home.
- People are afraid that others may criticize them or reject their goals.
- Mostly, people fear failure and disappointment.

HERE'S A POPULAR method to help you create an effective goal. It's called **S.M.A.R.T.** That means:

Specific, **M**easurable, **A**ttainable, **R**ealistic and **T**ime-oriented.

GOAL SETTING: A Money Making Attitude
Here are 5 benefits of goal setting for making money:

1   **Converts wishful thinking into reality.**
2   **Allows you to have more influence over your future.**
3   **Creates a focus and direction for your efforts.**
4   **Increases your odds of actually achieving your goal.**
5   **Helps you spot opportunities.**

Take a moment and come up with a couple of S.M.A.R.T. goals of your own.

_____

_____

_____

_____

AN EXAMPLE OF A S.M.A.R.T. GOAL:

I WILL OWN AN iPod™ within 8 weeks from today

GOALS

must be Specific. Goals such as happiness or success are too vague. So to be specific you must ask yourself "What exactly is it that I must do, want or have?"

GOALS

must be Measurable. Do I have the iPod™ yet? Is there enough money in the bank yet?

GOALS

must be Realistic. Even though it's a physical possibility for you to get your iPod™, is it likely that you can actually do the work and save up for it?

GOALS

must be Attainable. Given your ability to earn and save money, is it possible to actually purchase an iPod™? If not then you need to rethink your goal.

GOALS

must be Time-oriented. The reason for this is that it gives you a deadline. Secondly, it tells you whether you're on track to get your iPod™.

Now, ask yourself this key question: **Is what I'm doing on a day-to-day basis consistent with the direction I want to go and the goals I want to achieve?**

If you find that your day-to-day Attitudes and Behaviors are holding you back from your goals you can either:

A **Change your goals**
B **Change your day-to-day Behaviors**
C **Accept the frustration of knowing you're not living the life of your dreams.**

YOU OWE IT to yourself to avoid that last possibility, so why not have more fun and invest the time so that the first two are in sync? Here are a couple of ways to make it easier to achieve the S.M.A.R.T. goals you just set.

THE FOLLOWING WORKSHEET is called **My Success Game Plan** and it's an easy way of putting down all of the ideas we've covered so far in this book. We advise you not to write directly in the book but rather to use it as a master for photocopying purposes. A new photocopy should be used for the setting and achieving of each separate goal. You will be asked to identify why the goal is important to you. Knowing this will help you get through the times when you're tempted to spend your money on other things or you start to procrastinate.

THE LAST POINT is a statement of commitment and it's a very powerful tool to help you stay focused and on track. It is your goal, after all, and you owe it to yourself to be successful. By having a supportive friend, parent or teacher co-sign the plan you're giving them the right to hold you accountable so that you have the best chance of achieving your goal. You may return the favor by co-signing their **Success Game Plan**.

MY Success Game PLAN

I will achieve the following (S.M.A.R.T.) goal:

_____

_____

I will achieve this goal by _____ **(date).**

This goal is important to me because:

_____

_____

Where am I now, relative to attaining this goal?

_____

_____

_____

_____

How Will I Achieve this Goal - My ACTION steps

What beliefs/Attitudes if any will I have to change in order to achieve this goal?

_____

_____

What visuals can I use to help me connect with achieving this goal?

_____

_____

What obstacles & challenges will I have to overcome to achieve my goal?

_____

_____

Who could help me to achieve my goal?

_____

_____

What skills and knowledge will I need to achieve my goal?

_____

_____

_____

I commit to achieving the above Game Plan/Action Plan

_____   _____
Signature   **Supportive person's signature**

Attitude and Self-Esteem

EVERYDAY COUNTLESS MES-SAGES come in from family, friends, media, employers and schools. Over time these messages, both positive and negative, greatly influence your self-esteem. The higher the level of your self-esteem the more likely you are to succeed. The lower your self-esteem, the more likely that fears and doubts will stand between you and your goals.

BEFORE PROCEEDING WE would like to share with you one of our definitions. **Self-Esteem: The overall feeling that someone has about him or herself.** This feeling is the sum and total of all the positive and negative Attitudes that you possess. For example, you may be involved in dozens of activities, the majority of which are positive and only a few are negative. On the whole, you could be described as having a fairly high level of self-esteem. If you are not this person, if you have more negative than positive attitudes about yourself, if you have low self-esteem, are unhappy and would like to change things, here's what you can do.

THE FIRST THING is to avoid falling into the 'blame game' that occurs when you focus your energy on blaming other people for these negative messages. The reality is that it's your life and the key is to be responsible for the positive thoughts that you put in your mind. Here's what 'responsibility' means to us: It's about having the 'ability' to 'respond' correctly to any negative situation by saying **"It's not what happens to me that's important, it's what I**

Photo courtesy of the Ave Maria Foundation

TOM MONAGHAN

choose to do about it." Or "My past does not have to equal my future."

> "Failure is success if we learn from it." — Malcolm Forbes

TOM MONAGHAN'S LIFE is a good example of this principle. His father died when he was only 4 years old, leaving his mother to support his brother Jim and himself on her salary of $27.50 per week. For their own good she made the painful decision to put them both into a foster home. "When my dad died she took it very badly. She wasn't emotionally

It's important NOT to focus on what's impossible but to fantasize what's POSSIBLE.

equipped to deal with 2 young boys", recalls Tom.

"THE FIRST HOME was with a couple who didn't treat me very well. They criticized me a lot and I didn't do well in school. Then I was put into an orphanage that had its own school classroom. Sister Berarda was the teacher and I thrived under her guidance. She was firm but very encouraging and I became her star student. She asked me what I wanted to be when I grew up and I said 'a priest, a baseball shortstop and an architect.' The other kids laughed, but I was a dreamer. In fact, I daydreamed a lot when I was in school. I'd think 'I can't do much today because of the difficult circumstances I'm in but when I'm 18 I'll be free to do what I want'. As I got older the dreams usually involved growing a business."

"WHEN I GRADUATED from high school at 18 I was on my own with no money and just the clothes I was wearing. I took a job as a soda jerk [restaurant worker] that didn't pay very much but I got to eat for free. Then I drove a truck and took on all the overtime shifts that nobody else wanted because

Photo courtesy of the Ave Maria Foundation

couldn't afford to stay so I joined the marines because they said they would pay for my education."

"MY 3 YEARS in the marines were valuable for the discipline and training I received. It really helped me become a leader. I saved most of the money I earned but lost it all to a con man just before I got out. I went back to U of M but had to work at so many jobs to pay for tuition and books

that I kept falling asleep in class. Then I managed to buy a pizza shop for no money down, hoping to earn the money for college. The 'going to college' part didn't work out because it was so time consuming running the shop."

TOM'S STRATEGY WAS to sell the best pizza available, to deliver it hot and fresh within 30 minutes and locate near colleges and military bases. "It took a long time

Ranked in TOP 400 richest Americans

I needed the money to pay for college. For recreation I used to play ping-pong at the university's Newman Center. One night a grad student said to me 'The way you play I can tell you're very bright'. I don't know how my playing showed him that but I can't tell you how encouraged I was by that. It made me feel really special. I eventually got into U of M but

Photo courtesy of the Ave Maria Foundation

before we were really successful. I guess it was the feeling of the good times that got me through all the rough spots."

BY THE LATE 1970's, his chain of pizzerias, now called Domino's, had over 200 locations. Today, Domino's has a network of over 7,700 locations with more than 150,000 employees and sales of over $4 billion. "I believe that my faith has contributed to my goals in life. I have five priorities in life and they are: spiritual, social, mental, physical and financial. These priorities have guided me and hopefully will continue to do so."

"IN RETROSPECT it was probably the daydreaming that helped me the most. It's important not to focus on what's impossible but rather to fantasize about what's possible. I visualized about a positive future. I think you have to be enthusiastic about life and the opportunities you find. When you find something that excites you, follow it and be prepared to take some risks. And, don't ever quit. Everyone has a goal or dream in life and I believe anyone can achieve this if they set their minds to it."

TOM MONAGHAN ENCOUNTERED more than his fair share of setbacks along the way to success but he never let them discourage him. Forbes Magazine now ranks Monaghan in the top 400 richest Americans and estimates his net worth at $485 million.

Not bad for a DAYDREAMER!

Positive Affirmation Statements

Making Positive Affirmation Statements is a smart technique to replace negative beliefs with positive ones.

TAKE FOR EXAMPLE the story of **Yen** who, like most elementary school kids, loved to answer her teacher's questions in front of the class. Unfortunately, in her sixth grade she had a bad experience while presenting a book report on which she had worked very hard. She was trying to pronounce a difficult country name and kept getting it wrong. The harder she tried the more nervous she got and the greater her mispronunciation. This caused even greater laughs from her classmates. She ran home in tears that night vowing never to speak in front of the class again. When her turn to present came up again she declined until the teacher informed her that everyone had to present...no exceptions.

> **The harder she TRIED, the greater her mispronunciation which caused greater LAUGHTER.**

When forced to face the class, all she could think about was her last negative experience. It's no surprise that history and class laughter repeated itself. This negative belief about speaking in front of her class got worse over time.

LUCKILY FOR YEN her twelfth grade teacher recognized that she was a bright student who always did an excellent job preparing her assignments and that the only work that was needed was to help her change her belief about delivering class presentations. The simple, yet powerful positive affirmations that her teacher offered her were: "I am prepared for this presentation, I know my material, and I am a good presenter." Yen would repeat these three affirmations quietly many times a day to herself prior to doing her presentation. The result was that Yen, feeling more confident, delivered a much better presentation that resulted in her getting a B+ mark. This success confirmed the power of the positive affirmations technique. She used the same approach and got better and better in the classroom and eventually when speaking to groups of clients as part of her job.

ONCE YOU TAP into the power of positive affirmations, by changing your Attitudes and expectations, then you start the process of controlling your level of success. This applies whether it's the amount of money you have, how you perform in sports or the marks you achieve in a subject.

Seeing is Achieving— The Power of Visualizations

Visualization is a way of connecting to a goal by first creating a positive mental image of it.

HERE'S AN EXAMPLE: Josh loves mountain biking and hopes one day to be good enough to compete in the State championships. His parents are not rich and could only afford to buy him a second hand BMX. It's great to practice on but not the right bike for his purposes. He really wants the Trek Bruiser 3 mountain bike that he can get through a friend at a bike store for $800. He received $100 from his grandparents for his 13th birthday and, put together with his other savings, he's still more than $600 short of his goal.

> **He postered his room with pictures of his DREAM bike...they thought he was OBSESSED.**

THAT'S A LOT of money for him and it could have stopped him but he was sharp enough to adapt a technique he first learned from his swim team coach. She had studied sports psychology in

University and believed that proper fitness and plenty of practice was just one element necessary to win. She told the team "Mental conditioning is as important as physical conditioning in all aspects of life, including sports." The poster on her office wall screamed, **"When you can see It you will achieve It!"**

JOSH USED THIS technique to get his bike. He postered his room with pictures of his dream bike from various biking magazines as well as posters he got from his local bike shop. He used an image of the bike from the manufacturer's website for his screensaver, and had a picture taken of him sitting on the bike in a showroom taped to the cover of his school binder.

SURROUNDED BY THE visual image of his goal helped keep him focused on it. Whenever he was given his allowance or earned a few dollars working odd jobs around the neighborhood he was able to resist the immediate urge to spend the money on extras—fries, a new t-shirt, whatever—because his mind was focused on the goal of getting the bike. Some of his friends thought he was

becoming a little obsessed about it, but six months later he finally rode up on it. Then he started to enter and win local competitions.

Four Common Fears

1 **The person who limits him/herself because they're afraid to try.**

Denis tells the story of his friend Susan who is a high school Basketball coach.

A PASSIONATE AND caring educator, she noticed a junior who attended all the senior team's games and practices. At first she thought of her as just a fan or a supportive friend to someone on the team. But her infectious enthusiasm and her ability to read the play helped support the team's efforts. The next year at the team tryouts there she was again. Assuming she was there to be considered, Susan called her over and asked why she wasn't suited up. "Me…no I'm not trying out" Kelly laughed, "I'm too short." Susan responded, "What does your height have to do with

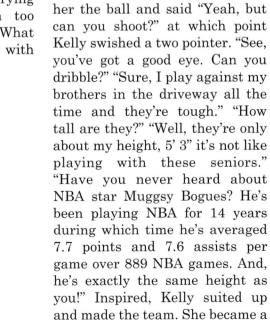

I'm not tall ENOUGH to COMPETE with these other girls.

it?" "I'm not tall enough to compete with these other girls. They're all a full head taller than me" came the reply. Susan threw her the ball and said "Yeah, but can you shoot?" at which point Kelly swished a two pointer. "See, you've got a good eye. Can you dribble?" "Sure, I play against my brothers in the driveway all the time and they're tough." "How tall are they?" "Well, they're only about my height, 5' 3" it's not like playing with these seniors." "Have you never heard about NBA star Muggsy Bogues? He's been playing NBA for 14 years during which time he's averaged 7.7 points and 7.6 assists per game over 889 NBA games. And, he's exactly the same height as you!" Inspired, Kelly suited up and made the team. She became a

valued player for the next two seasons and never undersold her talents again either as a player or in any life challenges. Whenever she came across any difficulties she remembered Susan's words of support "It's impossible to win in the game of life while sitting on the sidelines."

2   The person who is afraid to start a business because they're too young.

Missouri resident Bryan Heitman says "We had a computer at my house for as long as I can remember and I was always fascinated by it and what you could do with it."

WHEN I STARTED to see companies like CompuServe, AOL, Prodigy et al. starting up and the development of the Internet began, I was really interested.
BRYAN WAS 16 when he contacted **Gabriel Murphy**, a distant relative attending Cornell University. "He was the business guy, I was the techie. We were looking at all the other web companies starting up and thought 'Let's give it a shot.'" They pooled together $1,900, ordered an ISDN Line "and the business started to grow right away." Bryan says, "We loved doing it. The market was really interesting to watch and see it grow. In the beginning

it was a bunch of other guys like us who were passionate about what we were doing. Now it's been consolidated."

HAVING A GREAT idea is one thing but keeping it going when you need to expand can be difficult, particularly for teens. "It was difficult getting loans at first because we were so young and

were doing something non traditional. Banks were used to giving loans for traditional things like farms and real estate. We got the money eventually by showing

> ## It was difficult getting loans at first because WE were so YOUNG...

them the details of what we were doing. We had real numbers; real cash flow. We weren't financed by venture capital money; everything was financed out of cash flow. **I think kids really need to have good research to back up their plans and be able to answer any questions about the business."**

IN 2002 THEIR company, Communitech.net had $8,000,000 in revenues with a healthy 40% profit. Bryan and Gabriel sold the company in 2003, when Bryan was 21, for another very healthy profit. "I think the best way to succeed is to pick something you're passionate about. Don't go out looking simply to make millions of dollars but find a service you can provide that people are interested in."

I like the FREEDOM I have.

"I'M WORKING ON a couple of new projects now. I like what I do and the freedom I have. I work out of my house so it's a great lifestyle."

3   The fear of history repeating itself.

Many people grow up with nice surroundings in good neighborhoods and own computers and CD players. Others don't. Their parents can't afford better housing, let alone expensive toys.

The schools they attend can't afford the resources that others have come to expect. That can make getting ahead more of a challenge, but even that can be

Photo courtesy of NFTE

MIGDALIA MORALES

our own businesses and I just sat at the back of the class and thought 'whatever'. But the thing that impressed me was that, even though we were all pretty indifferent, they kept coming back. They didn't give up on us. Eventually I started paying attention and it got interesting but I didn't think it would do anything for me. I thought 'I'm just a kid, I can't run a business.'" It wasn't until she looked at her first business cards, for an office cleaning company she started herself, that she understood how much she had changed. "They read 'Migdalia Morales, President, Clean Sweep Cleaning Company'. I started to think 'Wow, maybe NFTE is for real'" she exclaimed.

NFTE
Teaching Youth to Build Businesses

overcome. Migdalia Morales, for instance, constructed a positive life out of the meanest of circumstances.

MIGDALIA GREW UP in a New Bedford housing project in Massachusetts. In her teens "...it was all about hanging out and trying to be one of the 'cool' kids. We were drinking and partying and never paid any attention in school. Growing up in the projects meant unemployment, drugs, teen pregnancy, AIDS and constant violence surrounded us. It's difficult to see that there is a world outside those streets. School just didn't seem relevant. I was constantly in trouble with teachers and it didn't phase me." Although she now lives in a better area, she still visits the old neighborhood. Unfortunately, not much has changed. "A lot of people I used to hang out with there are still doing the same old things, or they're in jail, or dead" says Migdalia.

WHEN SHE REACHED grade 12 Migdalia was bored, about to get kicked out of school and was looking for something different. "I heard about a program for teens called NFTE (The National Foundation for Teaching Entrepreneurship—WWW.NFTE.COM) and I was really skeptical. A couple of guys in suits came in and tried to teach us about starting

SHE STARTED TAKING more interest in regular school. NFTE helped her get into college while she was setting up and running several other businesses. "I had a candle making company and a graphic design shop. Now I have a landscaping business, Two

Brothers Landscaping, with my husband." Migdalia is thrilled with her new life as an entrepreneur. "It's the independence I love. Being an entrepreneur you get to set when and where you work. You're your own boss. You start to see opportunities that are all around you."

"ONE OF THE great things I learned from NFTE was to think outside the box. I was used to looking at the world only in terms of life within the projects and NFTE taught me to look outside the borders and see that there are other things and opportunities in the world. The other important thing I learned was to not give up. There are plenty of things to try. Sitting around drinking is, basically, giving up on yourself. You can do better. I mean if the highlight of your day is getting SO drunk you can't even walk, trust me, there are better things you can achieve. I see kids in the old neighborhood doing the same things and they think that's cool and they keep doing it until something tragic happens like someone getting killed. Then some of them wake up. There are so many talented kids out there that just don't have the resources. You have to look for them. You have to try the youth organizations or talk to your teachers. That may not sound like a 'cool' thing to do but many teachers can be mentors; they're not just there to teach."

"PART OF THE NFTE program is getting graduates like me to go back and teach the program in high schools to give back to the community. When I first started in the class I couldn't even stand up and talk and all of a sudden I was put in front of classes helping other kids. It totally changed me,

I'm just a KID, I CAN'T RUN a BUSINESS.

in a great way. I started to hear from parents who were thanking me because I had completely changed their kid's lives and that was really gratifying."

NFTE MADE A huge difference in Migdalia's life and it has been doing the same for thousands of others across America and around the world. They are a great example of mentorship. We'll share more of NFTE's story in the Resources Section.

4 The Fear of Not being heard.

One of the most common frustrations faced by the average teen is not being taken seriously by adults. Unfortunately, too many teens have accepted the old adage that "children should be seen and not heard."

AS WE SAID earlier if you buy into a negative belief such as this it will negatively affect your Attitude. How, after all, can anyone else take you seriously if you don't take yourself seriously? All the successful teen entrepreneurs we interviewed shared certain key characteristics. One of the most important is that they believe everyone has a voice...if they choose to use it. The following story illustrates the 'power' of using that voice.

FREE THE CHILDREN (HTTP://WWW. FREETHECHILDREN.ORG) is the largest network of children helping children in the world. In its 9

years of life it has been nominated 3 times for the Nobel Peace Prize. It was started by a 12-year-old boy, with no related experience, and a small group of his classmates.

Photo courtesy of Free The Children

CRAIG KEILBURGER

RENOWNED CHILD RIGHTS activist **Craig Kielburger** first became aware of the plight of the world's children while still a child himself. And it all began one ordinary weekday morning. Craig, then only 12 years old, was searching for the comic section of his local newspaper when a photo with a bold headline caught his attention. It read: "Battled Child Labour, Boy, 12, Murdered". Shocked, Craig read about the life and death of Iqbal Masih, a young Pakistani boy sold into slavery at the age of four. He learned that after spending six years chained to a carpet-weaving loom, Iqbal made a miraculous escape and became an advocate for the rights of enslaved children before his successes led a carpet-maker to have him killed.

"MORE THAN ANYTHING else, I felt angry", Craig recalls. "It was so unjust that Iqbal had to endure such horrific treatment and then be killed for speaking up, while I was lucky enough to be born into a great environment. I had seen suffering on television, in the newspaper, or even while walking past homeless people on the street. But like most people, I had learned to tune it out. We all learn to turn the page or change the channel. The injustice finally hit home for me the day I saw it through the eyes of another 12 year old."

DETERMINED TO TAKE action, Craig started to research the issue of child labour and began to discuss his findings with friends and classmates. "Normally I would have been terrified at the prospect of speaking in front of my class, but I was so angry about what had happened I just had to share Iqbal's story", Craig explains.

CRAIG'S COMMITMENT TO putting an end to child labour soon led him to found (Kids Can) Free the Children (**WWW.FREETHECHIL-DREN.ORG**). The organization initially began as a small group of students. "At first there were only 12 of us. In the beginning, our main goal was to raise awareness about the situation facing child laborers." This was to be far from easy. In the early years, the group struggled to convince skeptical and uncooperative adults that children could actually make a difference. "We tried to enlist the help of adults, but most were very unreceptive to our ideas. When we approached existing charities, all they wanted was for us to convince our parents to make a donation."

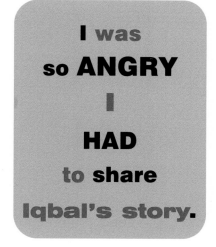

I was so ANGRY I HAD to share Iqbal's story.

SUCH SKEPTICISM MADE Craig and his friends all the more determined to show that children were capable of more. "We wanted to prove that children could help children", says Craig. "We started to make connections with other young people just like ourselves, and soon lots of us were writing letters to change child labor laws in different countries", Craig remembers.

TODAY, FREE THE Children is the largest network of children helping children in the world. The organization works to free children everywhere from poverty and exploitation by addressing its primary root cause, a lack of education. Its programs have now changed the lives of over one million young people in 40 countries. Thanks to the hard work and dedication of young supporters, Free the Children has built more than 400 schools that educate over 35,000 children, shipped over $9 million worth of medical supplies to those in need, and created primary healthcare centers that service more than 50,000 people. Alternative income programs have benefited over 20,000 people, and 200,000 school kits have

Photo courtesy of Free The Children

CRAIG HELPS THE KIDS

been delivered to new students around the world. "The organization works in conjunction with Oprah's Angel Network (HTTP://WWW.OPRAH.COM/UYL/UYL_LANDING.JHTML), and has entered into partnerships with organizations such as the United Nations. Although our organization has certainly grown, it hasn't really changed", Craig notes. "We still plan our actions one by one, only what began as a group of classmates from Toronto has now come to include thousands of young people from all over the world."

AMAZINGLY, CRAIG'S ACCOMPLISHMENTS don't end there. In 1999 the experienced activist co-founded Leaders Today, one of the world's top youth leadership training organizations. Craig's years of social activism have convinced him that we all have the power to make a difference. "I

believe that everyone has a cause or an issue that they're passionate about" he declares, adding, "I also believe that every young person has a gift, whether it's for sports or art, music or being a good listener. Whatever their gift, they can use it to raise awareness or funds to support a cause. They could organize a sports meet for charity, help a non-profit organization with website design, or start a letter-writing campaign. Too many people think the only way to help is by writing a cheque. That's just one way to support a cause. True philanthropy is not about money; it's about compassion and the action it inspires."

CRAIG IS ADAMANT that age should not deter anyone from social involvement, and believes that youth can actually be an advantage. "When I was 12, I thought my age was the only thing holding me back", Craig remembers. "I figured that everything would be easier once I was older. Now that I am older, I realize adults don't have all the answers, and I can see that they are often afraid to act. Young people have an advantage because they have the courage to take action."

CRAIG'S MOST RECENT project aims to encourage people of all ages to become socially involved. Together he and his brother Marc have co-authored a new book, Me to We: Turning Self-Help on Its Head. This inspirational volume empowers people to live the Me to We philosophy, which encourages volunteerism, service to others and social involvement. Craig hopes that his new book will do nothing less than inspire a new social movement grounded in community, caring and social responsibility. Judging by his own accomplishments to date, this is a revolution that has already begun.

Confident Expectations

There was a famous study done where researchers took an average group of teachers and gave them an average group of students.

THE TEACHERS WERE told they were part of an elite experiment and were selected for the study because of their gifted teaching abilities. They were also told that the students were hand-selected for their classes because they were extraordinarily bright. The teachers and students were asked not to discuss the experiment with anyone. By the end of the year, these classes had the highest grade point averages in the entire city! When the teachers were told that, in fact, their students were only average at the beginning of the year, they claimed the success of this experiment was due to their above-average teaching abilities. Imagine their shock when it was revealed that they had been picked precisely because of their average abilities.

BECAUSE OF WHAT they had been told, the teachers had a strong belief in their own abilities and that of their students. This dominant feeling produced a very positive environment, which produced the best possible results. This is known as Confident Expectations and it is another important element in creating positive Attitudes. We see countless examples of this everyday in all facets of life, in schools, businesses and sports teams, and we applaud those teachers, employers and coaches who recognize how essential it is to actively help the people they are leading to reach their potential.

YOU OR SOMEONE you know may have experienced this when a coach, friend, parent or teacher pushed you to go further than you thought you could go and you surprised yourself by achieving the goal. The best mentors can see your potential even when you can't. You think you're at your limit and someone is telling you 'you can go further'. And so you go further because you believe that. You overcome frustration, anger and weariness and you end up exceeding your expectation.

Photo courtesy of Michael Mahoney

MICHAEL MAHONEY

Your Past Doesn't Have to Equal Your Future

ONE OF THE biggest difficulties for anyone is getting stuck in the past. Too many people look to their past to give them clues as to what to expect in the future. But it's a trap: if you focus only on the past you will teach yourself to expect nothing better. We've heard tragic stories of kids who grew up in unspeakably bad homes who have ended up repeating a cycle of poverty and violence in their adult lives. But we also know the flipside: those kids who refused to be held back by their origins. Those who looked forward; who were determined to better themselves and build a positive life for their own kids. Theirs are some of the most thrilling success stories.

THE WAY TO create a better future is to learn from your past; accept it for what it was, then move on to deal with the challenges of today. Don't let your

past experiences—however bad they may have been—derail your activities in the future. Change tracks instead.

Michael Mahoney IS a survivor. He and his family over-came the scars of a terrible childhood to run an 'Inc. 500' company.

MICHAEL WAS THE oldest of six kids who grew up with an extremely abusive father. By the time he was two he was becoming aware of the extent of the extreme domestic violence he and his mother were enduring. It didn't

> **For years I couldn't TALK about the abuse, even to my closest FRIENDS.**

stop. "I knew he was bad and I had to deal with the brutal evidence of the abuse. My mother raised me to believe in myself. I could see the good in her as much as I could see the bad in him. Luckily I was a sponge for learning and I was determined to pull myself up and do better from a very early age."

THEY WERE LIVING abroad at the time when one of his sisters attempted to escape the climate of misery via suicide. Fortunately, she was not successful and their mother finally woke up and decided to leave. They relocated back to the U.S. where Michael had already set up an apartment. He had an accounting job at a large firm but another 6 mouths to shelter and feed was more than he could afford. In addition to tormenting them, their father also refused to pay any support, forcing the family onto public assistance and handouts.

MICHAEL REALIZED THAT if he and his family were to survive he was going to have to rethink his working life. He had always been an entrepreneur and that prepared him for what he needed to do.

"I STARTED A consulting business out of my bedroom. I cashed in my retirement funds and maxed out my credit cards. With $50,000 in debt, if I didn't get that crucial first client I would have been in serious trouble. But I had confidence in myself, I was determined, and read everything I could get my hands on. I learned from my mistakes. My first employee was my mother who saved my butt because she is so organized."

MICHAEL'S COMPANY, ADONIX, Inc., is one of the top suppliers of accounting systems in the Washington D.C. area. "In our first full year we grossed $886,000 and this year will top $4,000,000."

He has been a vocal advocate for the awareness of domestic violence issues for a number of years and is now on the Board of Directors for The Women's Center, (WWW.THEWOMENSCENTER.ORG) which provides shelter and support for women and families in need. One of his sisters went on to start her own business in graphic design, and was crowned Mrs. Virginia Globe 2004. She donated all her sponsor money to support victims of domestic violence (HTTP://WWW.WOMENINNEED.ORG).

"FOR YEARS I couldn't talk about the years of abuse, even to my closest friends. It's taken a lot of therapy to deal with it. My proudest accomplishment is that nei-

ther of my two kids has ever heard anyone yell or scream in our house. I'm proud to have broken that terrible cycle. My mom helped pull me through the tough times emotionally and I did the same for her financially. Our family has been blessed by God and turned things around. Our entrepreneurial spirit and our business has been a key driver." Michael is a member of the Young Entrepreneurs Organization (HTTP://WWW.YEO.ORG).

Teenagers spent $175 **billion** last year.

Negative Stereotypes in Advertising

ALTHOUGH WE ARE all individuals and responsible for our own decisions and choices, we do live in a community, however small or large it may be. The influence of that community on our Behaviors and buying habits is enormous. We are constantly bombarded by messages, many of which will help us make informed decisions on what to do or what to buy. Many people dislike advertisements and flip by them in newspapers and magazines or use the time between TV segments to scan other channels, go to the restroom or visit the kitchen. At its best, advertising attempts to educate us to the possibilities available to us as consumers. At its worst it tries to convince us that we can be happy only if we buy certain products or brand names.

MARKETING COMPANIES TARGET young people in particular. They describe teens as 'First adopters' which means that they will be the first to try out the latest technologies and fashions. Advertisers also know that if teens see their favorite artist or sports star using certain products that they are more likely to want to buy it. So, not surprisingly, they give stars

---

Exercise A

Go home and analyze any 5 ads from magazines, newspapers or TV for their messages. Look for some of the common advertiser tricks like the "Pain or Pleasure" concept. This is where they portray the most beautiful/cool kids using their products while the ones with the competing brands are alone and miserable. (Not surprisingly there is a lot of frustration when, after buying the product, their social status remains the same.) Write a brief description of what you think each ad/video is really trying to sell in the space below.

1 _____

_____

2 _____

_____

3 _____

_____

4 _____

_____

5 _____

_____

Exercise B

Write down the last 5 major purchases you made or intend to make (above $25) and try to determine what influenced your buying decision: saw it in a video, saw someone you admire wearing it etc.

1
_____

2
_____

3
_____

4
_____

5
_____

Exercise C
Now write down the last **5** minor **purchases** you've made and try to **determine** what influenced your buying **DECISION**.

1
_____
_____

2
_____
_____

3
_____
_____

4
_____
_____

5
_____
_____

enormous amounts of money to be shown with, or using, their products in photographs, videos and movies. The danger is that people start to equate their personal success with ownership of those products. Even worse, many who cannot afford to buy the latest fashion accessories or gadgets may start to see themselves, or allow others to refer to them, as "losers." This is a very expensive trap to fall into.

IF A MANUFACTURER makes a product that you think is well made and designed, something you will use and enjoy often, and you can afford it, by all means go and get it. If, however, you are buying that product only because you saw one of your idols using it or because you think your friends will like you more because of the purchase, perhaps you want to rethink it. You may want to spend some time discovering your own inner values and beauty. Ask yourself whether your friends like you for who you are rather than the things you own and the brand labels you wear. Then examine whether you really need a particular product or would be better off saving and then buying something later that may contribute more to your future happiness and success. If you really want to be a trendsetter, why not be the first amongst your friends to stop being seen as a profit center by huge companies and stars?

THIS IS SIMPLY a self-awareness exercise. It's your money, be aware of the reasons behind your spending. You may save a lot in the process.

Money Minimizers vs. Money Magnets

AFTER STUDYING WEALTHY and poor people for several decades around the world one key distinction has become abundantly clear to us. In our estimation there are basically 2 types of people. The vast majority of the population is what we refer to as Money Minimizers and the remaining 10% are Money Magnets. It's interesting to note that the Money Magnets have a combined wealth that exceeds the remaining 90% of the population. The core difference between these two groups is their Attitude to money.

MONEY MINIMIZERS WORK for companies where they're paid poorly relative to their efforts, and have no real job security. They can be replaced with little notice by someone willing to do the job cheaper. And there may be little or no job satisfaction. Money Magnets see the world differently. They want to control their lives and be in charge of what they earn by starting up their own companies; enterprises that are extensions of their own interests and passions. That's not to say that you can't be a Money Magnet if you work for someone else. Teachers and social workers are examples of employees who can achieve great satisfaction from their work. Millions of people love their jobs and enjoy working alongside other people to achieve a goal. What determines whether they are Money Magnets

Photo courtesy of the Orfalea Foundation

PAUL ORFALEA

or Minimizers is whether they have the right Attitude to take control of their financial future by making smart spending, savings and investing decisions now.

Paul Orfalea, THE founder of photocopy giant Kinko's Inc., comes by his entrepreneurial mindset honestly. Growing up in an extended Lebanese family he says, "None of my 300 relatives ever had a job, instead they all had their own businesses. My family were all terrific savers and everything had something to do with business. I remember once driving with my mother when she suddenly slammed on the brakes to check out the local fruit market that had just extended their hours to 24. At the time that was unheard of and my mother thought

it was brilliant. 'Look at that' she said 'they're amortizing all their costs over 24 hours rather than just the usual 10 hours'."

WHILE STILL IN college in 1970, Paul noticed long lines for the Xerox machine. Knowing that people waiting in line was a good indication of demand he started his own small photocopying busi-

> **Your Attitude towards MONEY, will ultimately ATTRACT or repel WEALTH.**

ness near the University of California at Santa Barbara. It started with a simple idea: provide college students with products and services they need at a competitive price. In addition to photocopies, he sold pens, pencils, and other study-related items. He even had his salespeople go into the dorms to sell notebooks and pens. The first space Paul rented for his copy business was so small the copy machine had to be lugged out onto the sidewalk. With extension cord in hand he literally took his business 'to the street'.

> **The space was so SMALL the copy machine had to be LUGGED out onto the sidewalk.**

NICKNAMED "KINKO" FOR his wild, curly red hair, Paul gave that name to his stores. It worked. He's turned his business into a huge international success with over 1,200 Kinko's stores worldwide. Wanting to relax and enjoy life and his family, the business was recently sold for $2.4 Billion dollars.

A MAJOR FACTOR influencing how Orfalea approached business has been the fact that he is dyslexic [impaired reading and

spelling abilities]. "I'm lucky, I can't read well," Paul states, and "I'm not mechanically inclined. I knew anybody else could do a particular task better than me, so I hired a lot of competent people."

"ENTREPRENEURSHIP IS ALL about asking questions. For so many business owners their past successes start to cloud their judgment. They start believing their own hype. I tried to stay out of meetings and the head office as much as possible. Talking with the front line co-workers is where you learn how a business is really working. If they're unhappy, then the business has problems. Some excellent ideas came from the individual stores. I was in a store once and noticed that they had done custom picture calendars from customer's own photos. It was a great idea and, extended throughout the chain, has made a huge profit."

kinko's

"I FEEL THAT the owner of any business needs to focus on three critical points: take care of your customers, motivate your workers, and balance your checkbook. It's really that simple." **COPY THAT!**

> **"Let us concentrate on the things which make for harmony and growth of our fellowship together."**
>
> — Romans 14:19

WHEN YOU HAVE an answer to each and every one of the questions on the next page, then, and only then, will you be fully ready to move on to the next chapter. Please take your time with these questions. The answers may be difficult for you. The more difficult they are, the greater your need to answer them. If you are willing to do this work, the other steps will flow easily and your potential for success at any almost anything will greatly increase.

Just to make **sure** that you are ready to **move** on to the next step, let's **review** what we've discussed in this chapter.

1 **For the purpose of this book what does the word Attitude mean?**

_____

_____

2 **How does your Attitude impact your ability to make money?**

_____

_____

3 **What is your definition of success?**

_____

_____

4 **What is your definition of wealth?**

_____

_____

5 **What is the point behind the phrase, "You can't hit a target you can't see?"**

_____

_____

6 **Why are some people more successful than others?**

_____

_____

7 **What role does responsibility have in your success?**

_____

_____

8 **What is your Success Game Plan for getting the things that you want?**

_____

_____

9 **What is the difference between a Money Magnet and a Money Minimizer?**

_____

_____

Behaviors for Making Money

now that you've worked on improving any limiting Attitudes to money, the next step is to make sure that your every action pushes you closer to your goals. There are millions of ways you can spend or invest your money and your time. If you choose wisely, you'll end up with more of both. If you make bad or ill-informed choices, you'll have neither.

> "The successful person is the individual who forms the habit of doing what the failing person doesn't like to do."
> —Donald Riggs

AFTER YEARS OF working with self-made millionaires, we started to notice certain common Behaviors. In this chapter we want to share some of the strategies that all successful people embrace as well as some of the ones they avoid. Clever people invest their time, energy and money so that they work smarter instead of having to work harder. That's not to say that they don't occasionally work long, hard hours, but when they do it's because they want to—not because they have to just to get by. Like with most things it's not about reinventing the wheel. All you have to do is choose the Behaviors that work best for you so you can achieve your goals.

ONE OF THE simplest strategies wealthy people use to build their money is to avoid being ripped off in the first place. They spend their money more effectively and then take the savings and turn that into wealth. Here are some ideas for saving money, which you can use to make more money through investments or building your own business.

Frugality: Make yourself rich, not someone else

MOST PEOPLE BELIEVE that the answer to all their financial problems is simply to have more money. The problem with this is that most people live beyond their means. They typically manage to outspend their income by between 5 and 10 percent. Proof of this can be seen in the fact that Americans are carrying the highest personal debt load in history—over 2 trillion dollars—and the total of outstanding credit card debt is the highest it has ever been and continues to grow.

The under 25 age group is now the fastest growing demographic filing for bankruptcy protection.

ALL WEALTHY PEOPLE know the value of self-discipline in their personal spending habits. They don't view saving as a painful process. Instead, they see it simply as delayed spending. Successful people realize that 'Until you have your own financial situation in order, the goal should not be to increase income, but first to live better and smarter within your existing income.' Everywhere you turn, someone is

tempting you to spend more money, and in fact the economy for the most part relies on consumers doing just that. The media is largely to blame for convincing many people that those who have money spend lavishly and that those who don't show the material trappings of wealth aren't wealthy. Did You Know: 75% of all US millionaires have never spent more than $199 for a pair of shoes. Think about the people earning minimum wage who are spending $150 for a pair of sneakers. Can they really afford it? Is it worth it?

MONEY MINIMIZERS CONFUSE income with wealth. Income is how much you make, wealth is how much you keep. Poor and middle class people spend their lives working for money to buy things that make them look like they have money and, as a result, they don't.

The Money Snapshot

HAVE YOU EVER wondered where all your money goes? You balance school, homework, sports and you work at a part-time job. You get paid and before you know it your money has disappeared. Most of us have some sense of what we spend our money on, but only by getting an accurate snapshot of our current financial picture can we pinpoint the places where savings and gains can be made. Take a photocopy of this chart; you

The ABCs of Making Money 4 Teens
Money Shapshot
Month: _____ of 20_____

Money In	Monthly Total
Part-time job # 1	
Part-time job # 2	
Allowance	
Business Income – Net	
Other	
Total Monthly Money In	
Money Out	**Monthly Total**
Expenses	
Savings (Remember, pay yourself first)	
Rent or Room & Board	
Telephone/ Cell Phone	
Internet	
Car Repairs & Maintenance, Fuel, Oil, Registration, Insurance, Parking	
Credit Card	
Loan Payment	
Groceries	
Eating Out	
Laundry & Dry Cleaning	
School / College Supplies	
Entertainment	
Tuition Fees / Course Costs	
Memberships	
Grooming or Hair Care, Toiletry & Cosmetics	
Gifts	
Church tithing	
Charity Donations	
Other	
Total Monthly Money Out	
Total Monthly Money In – less Total Monthly Money Out	

may want to use it again in the future. Take a couple of moments and fill in all the categories that apply to you. Once you've filled it in you will have an accurate picture of your financial situation. You can use the chart to identify areas where you can reduce your expenses, thus increasing your available money.

NOW, HERE'S THE most important part of the exercise: If you find a way to save $20 or more every month, put that amount into a savings plan so that it starts to work for you. Having completed this exercise it's time for the next step—your day-to-day spending habits. Here is a sample diary of how someone typically spends their cash. As you can see, it adds up quickly and

represents a substantial expense. Make some copies of the Daily Money Monitor and fill it in every night before you go to bed—it's much easier to remember if you do it every day—over the course of a week or more. These exercises work whether you earn $100. a year or $100,000. **It's not about how much you make, it's what you do with it that counts**.

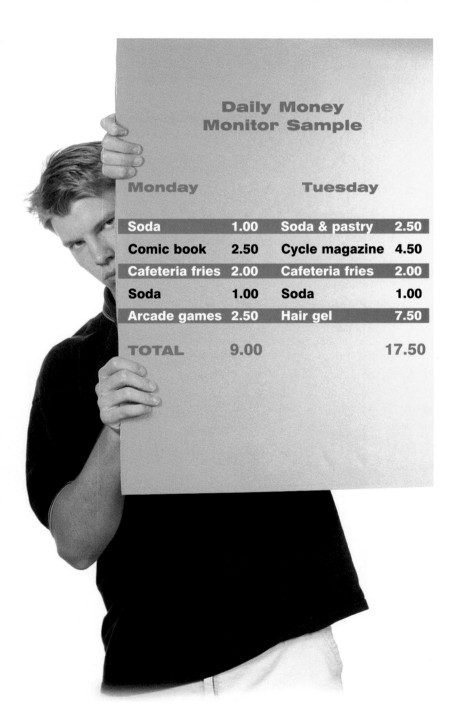

Daily Money Monitor Sample

Monday		Tuesday	
Soda	1.00	Soda & pastry	2.50
Comic book	2.50	Cycle magazine	4.50
Cafeteria fries	2.00	Cafeteria fries	2.00
Soda	1.00	Soda	1.00
Arcade games	2.50	Hair gel	7.50
TOTAL	9.00		17.50

It's **not about** how much **you make,** it's **what you** do with it **that** counts.

Daily MONEY Monitor

Monday	Expense	Friday	Expense

Tuesday	Expense	Saturday	Expense

Wednesday	Expense	Sunday	Expense

Thursday	Expense	*Notes*	

NOW YOU NEED to look at what you spend your money on and decide if it's all necessary. The point of the exercise is not to live without fun, it's to consider whether you could start to save for something you want by economizing. Do you really need the fries in the cafeteria at lunch? Maybe you could bring an apple from home instead. It would be way healthier and save some money. If you really feel you need them that's fine. Try and find something else you would be more comfortable eliminating. Again, the important thing is to make sure that the money you save goes into an account to build up for what you want to get in the future. In other words, don't just save the money then go spend it on arcade games.

Bring an apple from home instead.

Who Is More Important Than You?

FINANCIAL ADVISERS OFTEN use the expression "Pay yourself first." That means, when you earn money—before you allocate it to expenses or new purchases—always take a portion and put it into a savings account or investment vehicle for your future. It's about saving for a personal dream —whether that's going to college, a once in a lifetime trip, a car or a very comfortable future.

SOMEONE WHO REALLY understands this concept is Mississippi's Julialake Landrum. Although both her parents work in the financial services industry, Julialake is fully in charge of her future. Now 14, she earns money from babysitting, doing small jobs

Photo courtesy of Julialake Landrum

JULIALAKE LANDRUM

around her parent's office and at her grandparent's furniture store. She started her first savings plan when she was 11. "I started making money and I asked my dad what to do with it. He suggested that I open an 'aggressive growth' mutual fund. I started to read some of the books my parents had around and got really interested in things like 'The Rule of 72' [covered later in this chapter]. One of the books led me to a website with some calculators you can use to see how fast money can grow inside reputable funds [www.citibank.com has some free calculators in their "Planning & Tools" section you can play with, or try http://www.charterone.com/general/calculators.asp]. I showed this to some of my friends and they got really excited too. It showed how they could make lots of money and how little it takes to get started."

AMONG HER MANY other projects, she self-published a book called "Bathtime For Dixie." She paid a local artist to illustrate it and printed 150 copies at a cost of $700. "I sold the whole print run and made a $500 profit, part of which went into my mutual funds. Now I'm finishing up another book, a mystery novel for teens."

JULIALAKE HAS TOLD her story to lots of groups, done TV interviews and even spoke in front of 53,000 people at one of her parent's company's conventions. "I think growing up in the environment of my dad being in Primerica [Financial Services] really helped. His support and encouragement has been fantastic. Right now I put $100. every month into my mutual funds. That's a bit of a sacrifice because I'd like to buy other things, but it's going to be SO worth it in the future. I dream of setting up a Foundation to help orphans and the elderly and I have shorter term goals, like getting a law degree, which will take a lot of money. I really believe that if you start early, anyone can do it."

It's a bit of a sacrifice now it's going to be SO worth it.

> Go home and do this exercise with your parents. Fill in the chart below with the figures they supply. Not all columns will apply; approximate figures will be okay.

Monthly Expenses	Monthly Total
Rent or Mortgage	
Property taxes	
Electricity	
Natural gas/heating oil	
Water	
Groceries	
Telephone	
Cable/Satellite TV	
Internet	
Car payments	
Car Repairs & Maintenance, Fuel, Oil, Registration, Insurance, Parking	
Restaurants/Take out	
Laundry & Dry Cleaning	
Entertainment	
Grooming or Haircare, Toiletry & Cosmetics	
Pet supplies	
Church tithing	
Charity Donations	
Travel	
Other	
Total Monthly Expenses	

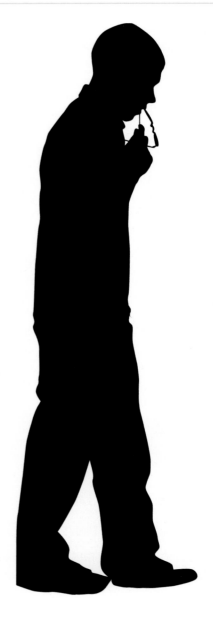

Bringing It All Home

DO YOU HAVE any idea what it costs to run a household? Although it may be many years in the future, someday you'll be setting up your own living space independent from your parents. Sure, it might be a great idea, but you should be prepared for the real costs.

NOW ASK YOURSELF how much you would have to earn—after taxes—to pay all those expenses. That great job at the clothing boutique or CD store may be fun, but how many of the above expenses would you have to eliminate if that job was your only source of income.

YOU'LL NOTICE THAT the biggest drain on your cash simply puts a roof over your head. If you were starting out on your own, that would be the first place to look for savings.

INSTEAD OF BUYING a home some people rent an apartment or, if they currently live in an apartment, they share the rent with friends. Let's go the next step. Pick an area you and your friends would like to live in. Then get a local newspaper and check out what it costs to rent a 2-bedroom apartment in that area. Call one or two and see what the rent includes. Does it cover the heat and electricity; laundry, parking?

What will you need in addition: a phone, cable, internet? Add up the total cost. What kind of job will it take to pay for everything? Remember, you'll still want to go out after school to restaurants and movies, and you'll probably want to have a cell phone or a car. All these things, you can bet, will cost more, **not less**, next year.

WE'RE NOT TRYING to encourage anyone to move out of their parent's houses, nor are we trying to scare anybody off. We just want you to understand what it really costs to run a household, and why your parents are always after you to turn the lights off when you leave a room.

You and Your Best Bud

THINK OF YOUR best bud. If you ignore them and fail to invest time with them, eventually they will be gone. However, if you visit your best bud often, respect them and take care of them they will never let you down.

WHO IS THIS best bud? Well in financial terms it's your budget. As discussed in chapter one there are two types of teens:
SPENDERS = MONEY MINIMIZERS
SAVERS = MONEY MAGNETS

These typical reactions fit the description of our Money Minimizers so we thought we would ask our friends and associates fitting the Money Magnets description to discuss budgets and got these RESPONSES:

- The lack of budgeting—not money—is the real issue
- It's YOUR budget; you can make it as rigid or as flexible as you want
- It only takes a short while once a week to maintain a budget
- Some of the most powerful budgets are the simple, straight-forward ones
- A budget is simply a plan to control future spending
- If you are committed to the budget, it can become a habit within 3 weeks
- What's more fun than planning to become wealthy?
- The ABCs Money Snapshot is easy and only took a couple of minutes

Learning to Stretch a Buck

"The way to wealth depends on two words, industry and frugality; that is waste neither time nor money, but make the best use of both."
— Benjamin Franklin

JUST dropping the "B" bomb is enough to send most adults cowering. The following is a sample of how most people react to the word "BUDGET":

- ☞ Budgets are for older people
- ☞ Budgets are not the issue, what I need is more money
- ☞ Budgets are too restrictive for my lifestyle
- ☞ Budgets are too time-consuming
- ☞ Budgets are too complicated
- ☞ Budgets require too much work and discipline
- ☞ Budgets are boring

Barter Instead of Bucks

Bartering is trading your stuff for someone else's with no cash involved. Abide by local tax rules.

Treasures Not Monsters Under Your Bed

Clean out your closet, under your bed, basement, attic and garage. Sell off things you aren't likely to use.

Frugality is in Fashion

When buying clothes shop mid- to end-of season. Fashions are still current but cheaper. Independent clothiers can negotiate up to 5% discount on cash sales rather than credit cards. Factory Outlets and retailers specialize in carrying brand labels at huge discounts. Try on the clothes and double check to ensure no flaws.

Money Down the Drain

Drinking purified water is good for you but at an average price of one dollar a bottle it becomes expensive. Save money by using one of the common, inexpensive

Life in the Fast Lane

- **Use public transport when it's a safe, available option**
- **Carpooling saves gas, parking passes and the environment.**
- **Use a bike rather than the car.**
- **Don't buy unnecessary options for your car. They cost more to buy, finance and repair.**
- **Slow down, avoid getting the speeding ticket and stay alive.**
- **Pump your own gas, its cheaper than 'full service'.**
- **Consider driving other people to school or work with you and share the costs.**

water filtration systems and refill your empty bottles for looking and feeling cool.

Financial Food for Thought

Eating at fast food joints can be fun but is very expensive and can do real damage to your health.

Keep track for a week of all the money you spend at fast food restaurants, vending machines and corner stores. Take this total and multiply by 4 to obtain your monthly total. You'll be surprised to see how much it adds up to. The hidden expense is the damage that the junk food is doing to your health.

A Prescription for Your Financial Woes

Ask your doctor for generic rather than full price medications. Everyone knows the health risks associated with smoking...you smoke, you die! The financial cost is huge; the average smoker could easily **save over half a million dollars**, over 30 years by simply investing the cost of the cigarettes in a mutual fund.

Run Over on the Information Highway

If you make long distance calls, get a decent long distance plan for your phone. Re-examine use of your mobile phone. It may be cheaper to have your whole family on a family plan than several separate cell phone plans.

Entertaining Ideas

Enjoy the latest blockbuster but try to make it on a Tuesday night when theatres in many communities offer a discount rate, or try going to a matinee and save money. The biggest money saver is to avoid buying the overpriced junk food on sale on the way into the movie.

IF YOU HAVE any interesting ideas on how other teens can save money, please email the authors at: **INFO@ABCS4TEENS.COM**

42

Start a classroom discussion on other creative ways to save money. Challenge other classes to come up with their own lists, then compare and swap ideas.

Be Street Wise—Don't Get Ripped Off

Over-Extended Warranties

ELECTRONICS. These are priced with such thin margins that the salesperson may make only a small commission on a sale. They can make much more if you buy the extended warranty insurance. Unfortunately the vast majority never get any value from this purchase. Electronic equipment tends to malfunction early in its life or very late. In the early stage it is covered by the manufacturer's warranty. If it makes it through the first year chances are it will make it until the point at which you would want to get rid of it anyway because it is obsolete or has been replaced by a newer version with more desirable features. The old adage 'you get what you pay for' applies to this category. Investing a couple of extra dollars in a well-respected brand will usually repay you with longer product life. Do some research into the brands with the longest life spans.

> "The only problem with debt is that you have to pay it back."
> — Patrick Morley

Car Warranties

Someday you may wish to purchase a new car. No car manufacturer is going to offer to cover an item that has a high probability of failure. Wear and tear items are not covered in the first place. The extended warranties only cover the things like the power train that will greatly outlast the coverage. Things like mufflers, suspensions, struts, shock absorbers, radiators, clutches tend to last through the initial warranty period only to fail when that period is up. Guess what's not covered in the extended warranty.

> **Many insurance salespeople will TRY to sell you over-priced life insurance.**

Life Insurance

You may not need this right now but sometime in the future you will be approached to buy insurance. The sole purpose of life insurance is to protect the income of the main money earner should they die. Life insurance is not an investment tool! The key to purchasing life insurance is to get the maximum coverage at the lowest monthly price. Only one type of life insurance does this, it's called Term Life insurance. Many insurance sales representatives will try to sell you over-priced insurance calling it an investment, these are usually called; Cash Value, Whole Life or Universal Life insurance, all of which are bad investment strategies. They benefit the insurance company and their sales force way more than you. Remember: Anything other than Term Life insurance is a rip-off. In fact, why not go home and ask your parents/guardian if they have either of these policies. If they do, suggest that they switch to Term Life. They will get much more coverage for a much smaller monthly premium. This one change can make a huge difference in your family's financial picture.

Taking Credit for Your Wealth

Minimize the number of cards you have to avoid extra paperwork and time wastage. You're more likely to fall behind on payments if you have multiple cards because you run out of time to organize the payments. Every time you are late on a payment costs you money needlessly. Never take a cash advance except in the most extreme cases such as you haven't eaten in a week. That is the most expensive money you can get.

> **Student credit card debt exceeds 500 million.**

43

Interest-Sting Comparisons

CREDIT CARDS ARE everywhere. If you don't already have one, check your mail; it will arrive soon enough. They are a convenient and low cost way of getting credit—if you use them properly. Used poorly, they allow companies to make huge profits from an often unsuspecting public. You don't want to be part of that group. If you need to buy something but don't immediately have the money, a credit card will delay the need for payment. Make no mistake, you still have to pay for your purchase, you just have a couple of extra weeks to do so. **If you really can't afford the item the best advice is: don't buy it until you can.** If you know you'll get the money from a job or an allowance or some other source that you can count on before the day the money is due, then you just got an interest free loan.

THE CRUCIAL POINT here is to pay off the debt on or before the due date on your monthly statement. If you don't pay off the full amount then the credit card company adds a charge to the bal-

They start charging INTEREST on the INTEREST charges.

ance. Some companies charge as much as 28.5% for this loan. That rate starts to apply to all further charges on the card, not just the original one that is now overdue. It gets to the point with some people that they are paying so much in interest charges that they can never pay down the original charge. Then, as if that's not enough, they start charging interest on the interest charges and that's when things start spiraling out of control. You can't afford to buy anything new because all your money has to go to paying off the growing monster of a debt. Companies make it worse by allowing people to make a minimum monthly payment, usually 5 or 10% of the total amount owed. You might think that this is the company's way of being nice—giving you more time to pay the

debt—but actually **it's their way of suckering you into paying them interest.** You see, they only get to charge interest—which is where they go from earning good fees to fantastic fees—when you take a cash advance or haven't paid off a balance. That's why they let you pay a minimum amount. Another trick they try is making the payment date at the end of the first week in the month. Their hope is that you will pay all your other monthly debts, like rent, school fees etc. and run out of money before you can pay off all of your debt to them, thereby starting the meter running on new fees. Beware also of the "Introductory offer" which entices people with a low interest rate. **READING THE FINE PRINT** will reveal that after 3 or 6 months the rate will revert to 18% or more.

UNFORTUNATELY, MILLIONS AND millions of people find themselves caught in these traps. Currently people are paying 80 Billion dollars annually in interest charges. We pay another 31 Billion a year in fees for charge cards. Yes, that's a lot of money. It can literally ruin a family, and it's almost always avoidable.

Another interesting point is that not all credit cards are created equal.

Do yourself a huge favor and learn what it costs to have a credit card. This one exercise could end up saving you thousands of dollars over time. Start by calling up or going online to find the annual rates for some of your favorite companies. Banks often offer different interest rates. They will usually have one around 18% as well as a lower rate card for which you'll pay a yearly fee. Question each carefully about extra charges. Some companies have recently moved to "No annual fee" cards but then add a monthly fee or a transaction fee per item to your card whether you pay off the balance or not.

Next, check with some of your favorite companies in the following categories. Ask them what rates and fees they charge to use and carry a balance on their credit cards.

	Rate	Low rate	Fees
My favorite department store	___%		$_____/mo.
Department store B	___%		$_____/mo.
Bank A	___%	___%	$_____/mo.
Bank B	___%	___%	$_____/mo.
Bank C	___%	___%	$_____/mo.
Gas	___%		$_____/mo.
Electronic department store	___%		$_____/mo.

Now let's compare the rates and see which one is the better deal. Assume you have to buy a new computer for $1,000. and can't afford to pay it off immediately. For this example we'll assign some typical rates. The "yearly rate" shows what happens as the debt starts to grow with compounding interest.

	Monthly Interest Payment	After One Year
Department store @ 28%	$ 23.33	$ 1,279.96
Bank A @ 18.5%	$ 15.42	$ 1,185.04
Bank B @ 16.5%	$ 13.75	$ 1,165.60
Bank C @ 7%	$ 5.83	$ 1,069.96

Here's an example of what happens at one national brand retailer if you pay only the minimum necessary every month for that computer.

Schedule of Payments For One Time Purchase of $ 1,000.00 with no additional purchases, monthly payments $ 50.00, interest rate 29.5 %

Month	Balance Owed	Monthly Purchases	Monthly Payment	Interest and Fees	Cumulative Interestand Fees
1	1,000	0	50	24	24
2	974	0	50	24	48
3	948	0	50	23	72
4	922	0	50	23	95
5	895	0	50	22	117
6	867	0	50	21	139
7	839	0	50	20	160
8	810	0	50	20	180
9	780	0	50	19	200
10	750	0	50	18	219
11	719	0	50	18	237
12	687	0	50	17	254
13	654	0	50	16	271
14	621	0	50	15	286
15	586	0	50	14	301
16	551	0	50	13	315
17	515	0	50	13	328
18	478	0	50	12	340
19	440	0	50	11	352
20	402	0	50	10	362
21	362	0	50	9	371
22	321	0	50	8	380
23	280	0	50	7	387
24	237	0	50	6	394
25	194	0	50	5	399
26	149	0	50	4	403
27	103	0	50	3	406
28	56	0	50	1	408
29	8	0	9	0	409

AT THE END of 2 1/2 years the computer is paid for. But it **cost you $409 to borrow that $1,000**. Ouch! How many hours do you have to work to earn $409?

And, this assumes that you made no additional purchases during that time, which would be unusual. If you do make another purchase, then you **immediately** start paying interest on that item and push off the date where you will be **debt free**.

Now let's look at buying the same computer on a low interest card and see what happens.

Schedule of Payments For One Time Purchase of $ 1,000.00 with no additional purchases, monthly payments $ 50.00, interest rate 6 %.

Month	Balance Owed	Monthly Purchases	Monthly Payment	Interest and Fees	Cumulative Interest and Fees
1	1,000	0	50	5	5
2	955	0	50	4	9
3	909	0	50	4	14
4	864	0	50	4	18
5	818	0	50	4	23
6	773	0	50	3	27
7	727	0	50	3	30
8	680	0	50	3	34
9	634	0	50	3	37
10	587	0	50	3	40
11	540	0	50	2	43
12	493	0	50	2	46
13	446	0	50	2	48
14	398	0	50	2	50
15	350	0	50	1	52
16	302	0	50	1	54
17	254	0	50	1	55
18	205	0	50	1	56
19	156	0	50	0	57
20	107	0	50	0	58
21	58	0	50	0	58
22	8	0	8	0	58

IT TAKES LESS than 2 years to pay it off and it only cost $58. We'd still prefer to spend that $58 on something more fun than interest, but you're way further ahead.

THE REAL PROBLEM is that a huge number of people are carrying balances of thousands of dollars on high rate cards and they may never be able to get out from all that debt. Even very smart people get caught in this trap so, go home and show your research to your parents and ask them what cards are in their wallets or purses. If they are paying high interest charges on a department store card, suggest that they get a low rate card from a bank and transfer the balance to that card. It will save them lots of money. If your information helps them out you may be rewarded with a bonus, like an increase in your allowance!

REMEMBER

Even a good rate is not as good as 0% which is what you pay if you use cash or make all your payments on time. Before you start building up credit card charges ask yourself if you really need the item(s) and if you really will be able to pay the amount off painlessly, before the due date.

ALSO KEEP IN mind "The X factor" which means that you can't always anticipate what curves life will throw you. You may be counting on getting paid from a job to pay off a purchase, then get sick and miss a few shifts.

Or you get an opportunity 2 weeks later for an amazing deal on something else that throws off your cash flow. A credit card is a very powerful tool. The winners among us know how to use it wisely, keep their spending under control, and are prepared for the unknown.

Behavior of Leveraging

WE HAVE ALL been blessed with a number of personal assets. They include time, energy, effort, money and creativity. There are three ways to make money; they all involve trading off one or more of our personal assets to get money in return. The more effective you are in this trade-off the greater the return on investment of your personal assets. In other words the more money you will ultimately make. We call this return on investment of personal assets "leveraging." The higher the degree of leverage, the greater the return, which means more money in your pocket and more of the freedom that comes with it.

THE MOST COMMON method of leveraging is called a job. In this case the personal asset people trade is their time, energy and effort in return for an hourly rate or salary. There are several key ways to maximize this form of leveraging. The first is to find an

The winners among us KNOW how to use credit cards wisely.

ideal job. A sense of passion for and connectedness to a good job will raise your overall satisfaction and will help you become more productive. The greater your productivity, the greater chances for higher pay. The second key to maximizing leverage is to constantly add to your skills, knowledge and experience.

THE SECOND FORM of leveraging is to trade money to make more money. This is called an investment. We will cover this in more detail later in this chapter. The final and most powerful method is to leverage your own creativity, and that means owning your own business. The third chapter of this book is dedicated to this strategy.

You need a way to STAND OUT.

How to Get a Job, Even if You Don't Have Much Experience

MANY PEOPLE THINK that the resume is what gets them the job. This is an over-simplification. Think of a job search like a baseball game—it doesn't matter how many times you get to third base, it only counts when you pass home plate. You get to first base by researching and identifying the best available jobs for which you are suited. Second base is achieved by writing a short letter introducing yourself and the top three reasons why you are perfect for the job. If this cover letter captures the interest of the employer you will move on to third base, which deals with the resume. An effective resume will detail any previous work experience, and provide additional information on school, sports, volunteer accomplishments, hobbies and interests. It's often not enough just to list your experiences and accomplishments on a resume. Sometimes it requires a little creativity. The fact is that **employers are often overwhelmed** by the volume of resumes that they receive, so you don't want your application to get lost in the crowd. You need a way to stand out. This is where creativity enters the picture.

SEVERAL YEARS AGO a young woman approached us after a seminar to provide her with some assistance in approaching a specific company for a job. She was about to graduate from a two year drafting course and had learned through her research that the most successful architectural firm in the city was looking to hire two junior draft people. She learned that the competition for the positions would be very high but despite her lack of formal job experience she was going to try her best to get the job. **We suggested that she try to learn more about the business issues** and challenges that confronted the firm and how she could be part of the solution. After several days of research she reported back that the new CEO wanted to instill a sales and customer service mindset throughout the entire firm.

ARMED WITH THIS information we suggested she make some modifications to her resume and portfolio. What we came up with was to take her resume and print it out on 'Blueprint' paper complete with a legend and drafting symbols. Her new resume was a personal brochure that told the story of her skills, knowledge and formal training but also showcased her talent and creativity. She then wrote her covering letter in the form of a sales letter, which she wrapped around the 'Blueprint' resume. The sales letter identified several specific areas that her skills, knowledge and personality would be of great value to the firm. She then packaged the sales letter and 'Blueprint' resume into a Blueprint packing tube and labeled it 'Blueprints for Your Hiring Success' and couriered it directly to the CEO. He was so impressed with the innovative approach he instructed his Human Resources manager to interview her for the job. During the interview she used a similar approach by converting the interview into more of a sales presentation. Needless to say she got the job, but she also negotiated the highest starting salary for any new graduate in that area. ◑

IF THE RESUME impresses the employer enough you will be invited to proceed to the final step, the interview. The interview is the home plate in the hiring game. It's a chance for the employer to get to know you as a person, to see how well you are likely to fit in with the team. Unfortunately, most people don't really "WOW" the employer because they are not sufficiently prepared for the interview. To help you get ready for your next interview we have made a list of 20 typical questions asked during an interview. Knowing this will help you prepare your answers in advance.

THE KEY THING to remember here is to not rehearse your answers to the point where you come across as being fake or plastic. It's in your best interest to relax and be yourself. One final note, be sure to describe yourself in an upbeat, positive fashion. However, always tell the truth, and never fabricate things. One of the biggest turn-offs for employers is false and misleading statements. In some cases false or misleading statements can provide the grounds for employee dismissal.

Take turns role playing both the interviewer and interviewee and get comfortable answering these questions. The rest of the class can provide valuable feedback on how well you handled yourself in the interview situation. Page 1/3

---

20 Typical Interview Questions You Need to be Prepared for:

Consider the following as you write your answers below:
☞ **Why each of the following questions would be asked?**
☞ **What insights about you are they trying to get?**
☞ **What answer would put you in a positive light?**

1   How would you describe your present/past supervisor?

_____

_____

2   What are some things your supervisors have complimented you on? What have they criticized?

_____

_____

3   What are some of the things you particularly like/ dislike about your job?

_____

_____

4   Why did you leave your last job?

_____

_____

20 Typical Interview Questions You need to be prepared for: (Cont'd) **Page 2/3**

5 **Why are you pursuing a future career as a ______________________?**

____

____

6 **Tell me about how you dealt with angry or frustrated people?**

____

____

7 **What is the biggest mistake you have made on the job and what have you learned from it?**

____

____

8 **What is your biggest accomplishment to date?**

____

____

9 **What school subjects did you enjoy most/least? Why?**

____

____

10 **What are your plans for further education?**

____

____

11 **How would you describe yourself?**

____

____

12 **What disappointments, setbacks, or failures have you had?**

____

____

13 What kind of situations make you feel tense and nervous?

_____

_____

14 What do you consider to be your greatest achievement? Why?

_____

_____

15 What are your hobbies and interests?

_____

_____

16 What special characteristics should I consider about you as a person?

_____

_____

17 What do you feel are your personal limitations?

_____

_____

18 How do you deal with disagreements with others?

_____

_____

19 What can you do for us that someone else can't?

_____

_____

20 Why should I hire you?

_____

_____

ANOTHER POINT TO consider is that the majority of employers make up their mind about the job-seeker during the first 30 seconds of the interview. We have all heard the old expression, **"first impressions count"** well it's particularly true in an interview. How you are dressed, your body language, level of enthusiasm and manner of speaking will greatly influence your chances of landing that job. The idea is not to show up wearing a tux and sounding like a college English Professor, but to **dress cleanly and appropriately** for the job. You can take your clues by watching other successful people in similar jobs to discover how they act and dress.

Sources of NETWORKING:

- Friends
- Family
- Teachers
- Coaches
- Community Leaders
- Religious Leaders
- Local Business Owners
- Volunteer Organizations

WHERE TO FIND JOBS

GUIDANCE COUNSELOR
Most high schools have a guidance counselor or a career officer. These people can be a great resource in letting you know about various job opportunities.

STUDENT EMPLOYMENT BULLETIN BOARD
Often job postings can be found on Student Employment Bulletin Boards, which are normally located in the hall beside the Guidance Counsel Office or the Administration Office.

COMMUNITY MESSAGE BOARD
Virtually every community has at least one Community Message Board. The typical locations for these boards are: local shopping centers, public libraries, community centers, youth centers, Town Hall and churches. Not only can you find job listings but you can often offer your services by placing your own notice on the board.

LOCAL NEWSPAPER JOB LISTINGS
One of the most commonly used methods by employers is the listing of available jobs in the local newspaper.

HELP WANTED SIGNS IN WINDOWS
Check out the windows of the shops downtown or at your local mall, and you may be surprised at how many businesses are currently hiring. This also provides you an excellent opportunity to check out the business to better understand what the job is all about.

INTERNET
The most important new tool for hiring is the Internet. Employers either post "available positions" on their organization's website or they subscribe to an online recruiting company like Monster.com or Yahoojobs.com. There are also hundreds of smaller online recruiting services.

NETWORKING
Finally, the most common method employers use to hire people is word of mouth, which we'll call networking. Simply said, networking is talking with people you meet and discussing points of mutual interest. As a result of these discussions you can learn about various job opportunities, find out what the work is like and about the personality of the employer. With this information you are better equipped to land the job.

HERE are a COUPLE of things to remember about networking:

☞ **Don't be afraid of people. The worst they can say is "No."**

☞ **Always be polite, positive and never speak badly of others. Not only is this the way 'your mama brought you up' but you never know when you may have to deal with this person in the future.**

☞ **Don't waste people's time; be clear about what you want.**

☞ **The point of networking is the mutual social exchange of ideas and contacts, so ease-up on it.**

☞ **Don't "hard-sell" people.**

☞ **Don't back people into a corner. If they don't show any interest, thank them for their time and move on.**

A.N.D.

Ability The ability to pay the employees' wages

Need The real need to hire someone

Desire The desire to have you be the one hired

THE FIRST TWO elements, Ability and Need, cannot be created by the job applicant—they must already exist within the potential employer. Your task is to do the research to locate the various local employers who have these two things—they need you and they can pay you.

THE KEY TO relationship selling is for you to focus on building the employer's desire to hire you over all other applicants. The rest of this section focuses on how to better present yourself.

Your Ideal Job is Just One Sale Away

WE BELIEVE THAT selling is just a form of communications. In fact our definition of selling is **"The art of influencing or persuading someone to your way of thinking."**

WHEN YOU EXAMINE sales, you quickly realize that everyone sells something or other every day. For instance, take two friends who are trying to decide which movie to go see. He may be interested in the latest action flick, while she is dying to see a new comedy that everyone at school has been chuckling about. The best "salesperson" will influence the other and thus determine which movie is seen. Think about getting a job. Isn't the applicant trying to persuade the employer that they are the best person for the job? **People that know how to "sell themselves" effectively get the job!**

PEOPLE RARELY DEVELOP their selling skills because in most cultures selling has a bad reputation. When you mention sales to the average person they normally see this as a negative process, something that you do to someone. Stereotyped images of manipulative, slick, pushy and sometimes even dishonest "used car salesmen" will come to mind. The reality is that sales—like any profession—has both honest and dishonest players. The act of selling is neutral, it is neither positive or negative. What makes the difference is the intentions of the person. Are they trying to gain something at the expense of the other person or focusing on a true win-win situation? The professional, high integrity salesperson believes that selling is something you do with someone, not to someone.

THE BEST WAY to look at sales is the Relationship Selling Method. In order for the potential employer to "buy into" you as a future employee, the following three elements must be present (A, N, D);

Proving Your Point with Reference Letters

ONE OF THE best ways to back up the claims you make on your cover letter or resume is to include reference letters from people who can vouch for your abilities, track record and character. These letters can come from teachers, coaches, neighbors, religious leaders and former employers.

Negotiating

PRIOR TO APPLYING for the job, part of your research should have uncovered whether the wage is fixed or flexible. In some cases the wage offered for the job is fixed, meaning that the specific wage rate was determined in advance and it won't change. Once the employer has decided that you are the person that they want to hire it would be unwise to try to ask for a higher wage. However, there are many cases where the

Let the employer make the first wage offer.

wage rate is flexible; it is these opportunities where the job seeker's negotiating skills can really pay off. It's a good strategy to allow the employer to make the first wage offer for two reasons: one, you might have suggested a lower amount, and two, you now know an amount that the employer is prepared to pay. At that point you can counter with a higher wage and allow them to counter with a new amount. This can continue until both parties feel an acceptable amount has been agreed upon. This also applies to negotiating bonuses and commissions

**DENIS & ALAN'S
6 RULES OF NEGOTIATING
(and how they relate to the job search)**

RULE # 1
BE INFORMED & REALISTIC

You can't have too much information when going into a wage negotiation. Information equals power. Understand the dollar value of the job as it compares to similarly paid jobs in your area. Be realistic in understanding the reasonable amount of money that this employer can pay for the job.

RULE # 2
KNOW YOUR STRENGTHS AND SELL YOUR VALUE

What competitive advantages do you have over the other applicants? Why should the employer hire you at your desired rate?

RULE # 3
COMMIT TO A WIN/WIN PHILOSOPHY

Why is hiring you at this wage in the best interest of both parties? What can you do to ensure that you reach a win/win deal?

RULE # 4
DON'T JUDGE A BOOK BY IT'S COVER

Never underestimate the abilities or negotiating power of the other person. The moment you begin to underestimate them is the moment that you start to lose.

RULE # 5
DRAW A LINE IN THE SAND

Know your boundaries prior to starting the negotiation process. Have an absolute minimum wage that you will accept, the bottom line you will not compromise. If they're offering less, you should be prepared to walk away, with no hard feelings.

RULE # 6
LEARN FROM THE PAST

Review how well you have performed in previous negotiations. What could you do differently next time? How can you improve both the bottom line and the relationship?

NOTE

The principles we have covered in the Networking, Selling and Negotiating sections of this chapter apply equally to getting a job or to being an entrepreneur.

Volunteering

ONE OF THE greatest challenges in starting out is that to get a good job you have to have some experience. But if you can't get hired, you can't get the experience. So what do you do? Often the solution is to do some work for free. By volunteering your time and energy, you have offered a low-risk opportunity to a prospective employer to observe you in action. After a time, if a position opens up, you'll have a head start. Volunteering can be fun if you are making a meaningful contribution to a good cause you're passionate about. If that's not reward enough, volunteering is also a great way to "test the waters", to learn about a variety of career options, all the while building skills and knowledge. This makes your resume stronger and makes you a more marketable job applicant. Volunteering offers networking and travel opportunities for those who want to experience the real world. In some schools volunteering can earn class credits.

> "You can tell what they are by what they do."
>
> — Mathew 7:16

VOLUNTEER ORGANIZATIONS

ACTION
1100 Vermont Avenue, N.W.
Washington, DC
20525

4-H COUNCIL
7100 Connecticut Avenue
Chevy Chase, MD
20815-4999
Telephone: 301.961.2800
www.fourhcouncil.edu

CANADIAN 4-H COUNCIL
1690 Woodward Drive,
Suite 208
Ottawa, ON
K2C 3R8
Telephone 613.723.4444
www.4-h-canada.ca

NATIONAL VOLUNTEER CENTER
111 North 19th Street,
Suite 500
Arlington, VA
22209
www.1-800-volunteer.org
Telephone 703.276.0542

UNITED WAY OF AMERICA – YOUNG AMERICA CARES
701 North Fairfax Street
Alexandria, VA
22314
www.unitedway.org
Telephone 703.836.7100

YOUTH VOLUNTEER CORPS OF AMERICA
1080 Washington Street
Kansas City, MO
64105-2216
www.yvca.org
Telephone 816.474.5761

David Battey is an example of someone who started volunteering at an early age. When he was 14, through his church in Kansas City, he started tutoring fifth graders and coaching sports. In 1986 he founded Youth Volunteer Corps. "I knew teenagers could make a difference; they just needed more ways to do so," says Battey. YVC's Mission Statement is this: To create and increase volunteer opportunities to enrich America's youth, address community needs and develop a lifetime commitment to service.

CURRENTLY THERE ARE 49 sites throughout America and Canada involving projects as diverse as tutoring elementary students, serving meals to the homeless, removing graffiti, painting murals, creating web pages for non-profit agencies and taking children with disabilities on horseback rides. In 2004, over 41,000 youth were actively involved in the programs.

> I knew teenagers could make a difference, they just needed more ways to do it.

HE SUGGESTS THAT people need to know as much as they can about the field of business they're interested in as early as possible—you can never start too soon. He warns young people: **"Don't let the fact that you are young hold you back from pursuing your business dreams.** Being young provides two great advantages, 1) your level of enthusiasm and 2) the fact that you probably don't have too many financial obligations, unlike people in their 30's and 40's. You require less cash flow thus providing a greater chance that the business will succeed."

Photo courtesy of YVCA

YVC VOLUNTEERS MAKING A DIFFERENCE

IF YOU CAN put yourself in an employer's shoes and understand his or her needs, you will be better able to communicate your value as a prospective employee. Take a few moments to fill out this **quick exercise**. It will provide you with some insights into which of the highly valued employment traits you currently possess and those you wish to further develop.

The ABCs of Making Money 4 Teens
My Employability Quiz

Instructions: Circle the number that comes closest to representing how true the statement is for you right now (a rating of 1 would represent never true, while a rating of 5 would represent always true).

Statement	Rating
I have a proven ability in selling stuff.	1 2 3 4 5
I enjoy serving others.	1 2 3 4 5
I have demonstrated the ability to cut costs.	1 2 3 4 5
I find ways to do more things faster without compromising quality.	1 2 3 4 5
I am punctual and honest, people can count on me.	1 2 3 4 5
I am successful at organizing projects.	1 2 3 4 5
I am a true team player.	1 2 3 4 5
I can find productive uses for old/discarded items.	1 2 3 4 5
I can lead a team in delivering great results.	1 2 3 4 5
I have a positive influence on my co-workers/ team mates.	1 2 3 4 5

Interpretation: A score of 5 in any statement demonstrates an area of strength that is highly valued by today's employers.

Questions to consider:

What type of job requires my talents?

_____

_____

What other jobs/ opportunities should I investigate further?

_____

_____

What other areas should I choose to develop further to make myself more employable?

_____

_____

Investing

EVERYBODY IS AN investor... whether they know it or not. We all invest our time in educating ourselves, both to broaden our experiences and to improve our chances of landing more interesting and better-paid employment. We invest time in our families, our hobbies, our volunteer efforts, our sports. Financial investing is actually easier than all of the above, because you're not doing the work—the money is. In this section we want to show you some of the basics. They are simpler than you might imagine. And using them can make you a lot of money with virtually no effort.

> "The greatest mathematical discovery of all time is compound interest."
> — Albert Einstein

Free Money – The Gift of Time

A LOT OF people assume that becoming a millionaire involves a lot of work, a lot of luck or a huge amount of money to start with. This is not true. If you were to set aside $25 every week from the time you were 21 and invested that money in something like a mutual fund which earns an average of 10% you would have over a million dollars in your account when you turned 65. Now, we know 65 is a long way off, but think about it. **Simply by transferring a small amount of money every week from the hands of a fast food supplier to a broker**, you become a millionaire without doing any work. That's the magic of compounding.

THE TRICK WITH compounding is that it starts off very slowly, then over time, like a snowball rolling downhill, builds to the point where your principal amount literally starts to double every few years.

Let's go back to the example of the $25 weekly investment started at age 21. That earned you an amazing $1,056,986. Now, if you had started that plan at age 16,

those extra 5 years of compounding would make your account swell to $1,693,893. In other words, **the cost of waiting 5 years** to start saving cost you $636,907!

OF COURSE, NO one will blame you for not wanting to divert $25 every week when you're 16 years old, even though that $1,693,893 is pretty appealing. You want to buy clothes, DVDs and have fun with your friends. OK, fine. How about agreeing to start that savings plan when you're 21 but also agreeing that when you reach, say, 25, and are earning more money, you will start diverting $50 every week to your fund. That would help you catch up and result in a total of $1,650,895.

The Rule of 72

THE SECOND CRITICAL element of any fixed investment (stocks work differently) is the rate of interest (or profit) it will yield. The higher the rate of interest, the better your return (profit). That's common sense. But to fully appreciate the impact that interest rates have on your future wealth let's look at **"The Rule of 72."**

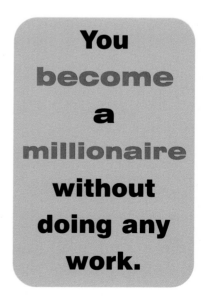

You become a millionaire without doing any work.

The Rule of 72 states that your money will double at an approximate point determined by dividing 72 by the rate of interest.

THE FOLLOWING CHART illustrates this phenomenon.

THE RULE OF 72 IN ACTION.

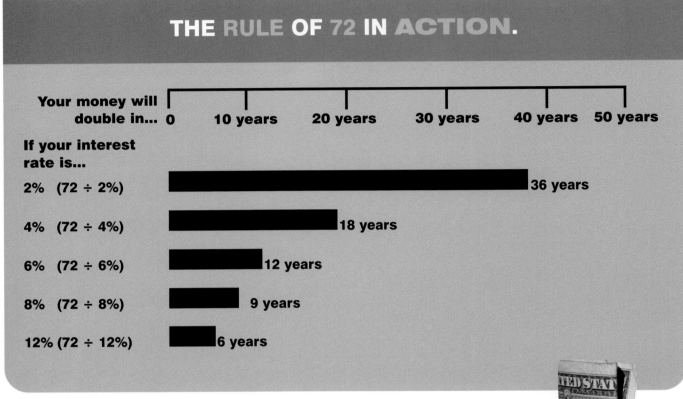

Your money will double in...	0	10 years	20 years	30 years	40 years	50 years

If your interest rate is...

2% (72 ÷ 2%)	36 years
4% (72 ÷ 4%)	18 years
6% (72 ÷ 6%)	12 years
8% (72 ÷ 8%)	9 years
12% (72 ÷ 12%)	6 years

SO, IF YOU invest $100 in an account that pays you 2%, you will double your money in 36 years. If you invest that same $100 in an account that gives you an 8% return, your money will double in only 9 years. **Quite a difference!** Remember that higher rates often come with higher risks. **Please check this out with a trusted, knowledgeable adult before you make your investment.**

> **"Those who understand compound interest are destined to collect it. Those who don't are doomed to pay it."**
> — Tom and David Gardner

Photo courtesy of Lesley Scorgie

LESLEY SCORGIE

A Million Good Reasons To Save

Lesley Scorgie really understands the power of saving and investing and, luckily for her, did both from an early age. Having adopted the 'saving' mindset at age 10 will pay off for her when she becomes a millionaire shortly after she reaches her 25th birthday! The best part about her story is that she has done nothing extraordinary or anything that virtually any other teen can't do.

"I GUESS I first started getting interested in money while reading books by Jeffrey Archer. His stories involve lots of entrepreneurs and I was interested in how these 'rags to riches' stories came to be. Then I started reading magazines like Fortune and Forbes. When I was 10 I started buying Savings Bonds with money I received on my birthday and from a job delivering flyers."

I GOT MY first part time job when I was 14 and decided to put half of everything I earned into savings vehicles. I guess that makes me a bit of an anomaly. It may be it bit unusual for a kid to think that way but I know that by saving now, I'll end up with a lot of money in the future and it will be well worth it. But, I'm not really giving up all that much anyway. I have lots of friends and still buy CDs and lots of stylish clothes; I just wait till the clothes are on the sale racks before I buy them. I don't blow money on junk."

IT'S IMPORTANT TO get the savings mindset. If, for example, you save your allowance you may be able to get a bike at the end of the year or, if you keep saving, a Lamborghini when you're 25! I

tell friends that if your parents give you $20, put half of it in a savings plan like a mutual fund. You can still have plenty of fun with the other $10. The important thing is not how much you have it's what you do with it that counts. It's about budgeting and knowing whether or not you really need something before you go and get it. If parents don't have good savings habits then it will be tougher for their children to acquire them, but if children learn it can rub off on their parents.

MY GOAL WAS to be a millionaire when I reached age 25. Now I'm 21 and in my 4th year of university. School was more expensive than I originally thought so it will be a little longer before I reach my goal but it was well worth it. **Education's expensive but it's an investment, not a cost**, and I'll leave college debt free thanks to my savings."

> **I'll leave college debt free thanks to my savings.**

"IT'S A MATTER of a little 'delayed gratification'. I still have everything I need but I'll have even more in just a few years."

Savings Vehicles

IT WOULD TAKE an entire book to explore the many ways you can save and invest your money. This is not that book. What we will do is give you the basics. If you're not interested in this section right now, keep it for a few years, when the information in it may be much more useful to you. If you want to know more, check out our last book **"The ABCs of Making Money"** or look in libraries and bookstores under Personal Finance.

THE BOTTOM LINE on investing is that the **amount** you invest is not the key to building wealth. The key is to **start making a regular contribution**. Even if it's only $5 every week, it gets you

> ## A savings account is a step up from a cookie jar.

into the habit of saving for your future. Then, as you get older and start earning more money, it will be very easy for you to increase your investment from $5 every week to $10 or $20 or more. Trust us, the easy part will be finding

the money. Your real challenge is to set up a plan and make it a habit to contribute every week, or every time you get paid. If you do this now, or at least before you hit the age of 20, over time you will thank yourself for doing this and consider this one of the most valuable books you ever read!

THE LIST ON the following page starts with the safest places to invest your money and increases in risk the further down the list you go. The less risk you're willing to take the less you generally earn **(remember the Rule of 72)**. The higher the risk, the higher the payouts can be, though you have to be prepared to lose it all if there is a market meltdown or a company goes out of business.

SAVING VEHICLES

SAVINGS AND CHECKING ACCOUNTS

A savings account is a step up from keeping your money in a cookie jar because it is safer. Through the Federal Deposit Insurance Corporation a deposit of up to $100,000 is guaranteed by the U.S. government. Caution: Make sure that your financial institution is covered by the F.D.I.C. and, if you live outside the U.S., check your financial institution's deposit protection system. The savings account typically pays a very small amount of interest. The benefit here is that your money is available at almost any time you need it. A checking account allows you to easily distribute your money to other people by writing checks, with the added security of not walking around with cash. Typically you will pay fees for using your checks and the interest rate will be very small.

CERTIFICATES OF DEPOSIT (CDS)

This is a fully guaranteed method of saving that pays higher interest than savings or checking account rates. It is locked in for an agreed period ranging from 30 days up to five years which means that you make more profit but you can't get your money back until the end of the term you've agreed to take.

T-BILLS

Treasury Bills are government IOUs issued for a term of one year or less. You do not receive interest; rather they are purchased at a discount. For example, you buy a $10,000 one-year T-Bill for $9,400. The minimum amount you can purchase is $10,000 with increases of $1,000 thereafter. Again, you make a bit more money but you can't get your money, if you need it, until the agreed time is up.

GOVERNMENT BONDS

You are loaning money to the government, which they will pay back at a predetermined time and rate of return. Some governments offer a tax incentive tied to the issuance of bonds.

MONEY MARKET MUTUAL FUNDS

This is a higher-yielding investment which is not guaranteed but is still very safe because of its conservative nature and the stability of capital. Mutual Funds allow thousands of people to pool their investment money. They are managed by dedicated portfolio specialists.

STOCKS

With stocks, you are purchasing shares of ownership in a corporation. You share in both its profits and losses (remember Enron?). You can make money from stocks either by selling them at a profit, or receiving regular income from them in the form of dividends.

MUTUAL FUNDS

Allow you to pool your money with many others to invest in a broad range of securities. They are managed by experts who carefully monitor the performance of the investments in their specific portfolios, allowing you to sleep at night while they track the markets. In theory these "experts" will do a better job than most in picking the better-performing securities. However they do make mistakes. Some smart investors pay less attention to the make-up of the portfolio and more to following successful managers from fund to fund. Most mutual fund companies advertise themselves as no load, which means that you pay no upfront fee to purchase them. Back-loaded means that you pay a fee when you sell the fund unless you keep your money in

for a specific amount of time, typically three to seven years. That does not mean these are the only fees you pay. Remember, there is no such thing as a free lunch. All funds have a Management Expense Ratio or MER. This is the amount the company charges for administering their funds. These fees come off the top and typically hover in the area of two per cent. So, if your fund says it returned six per cent this year, it actually made closer to eight

per cent before the management took its fees. Even if your fund returned only one per cent, or if it lost money, the company still took its fee. Whoever sold you the fund also got paid out of this expense charge. There are some funds that charge very low fees, from one to one and-a-half per cent, and can afford to do so because they avoid the expensive advertising campaigns. These are, by definition, harder to find. They may deal only with portfolios of $25,000 and above. For most people, who do not want to become financial experts, investing in a 'Blue Chip' mutual fund would be a fairly safe bet with a consistent gain.

INDEX FUNDS

A sure way to avoid making fund companies and their sales staffs rich from your money is to invest in Index Funds. With an Index Fund you purchase small pieces of a large number of companies. The S&P 500, for example, is a

grouping of 500 large company's stocks, which account for something like 80 per cent of all stocks traded in America. The index measures their collective performance. Another popular index is the Dow Jones, which measures the stocks of a narrower group of 30 active, large companies. So, if you invest in the Dow Jones' Index, you're buying a piece of those 30 companies.

The management team of an Index Fund is a computer, which costs much less to maintain than a group of Harvard business graduates. The upside of an Index Fund is the low fee and returns which, on average—though not always—outperform the highly paid experts. The downside is that there is nobody watching on your behalf for a 'meltdown' or market correction. Index funds are not great performers in "bear markets", those cautious, slow markets that occur most typically when the economy is in recession, or close to it. An actively managed Mutual Fund will certainly cost more but it MAY be better equipped to see a meltdown or correction coming enough in advance to rebalance the fund to protect your money, or it MAY react quicker once any market troubles begin. Lots of fund managers do neither. If you are in for the long haul, putting part—not all—of your portfolio in an Index Fund is a great, low-cost bet.

DOLLAR COST AVERAGING

Most first-time investors simply don't know when the best time is to enter the market and start investing. In the Dollar Cost Averaging method, you put the same amount of money into an investment each month. As the price of the investment rises and declines, you end up purchasing more shares when prices are low and less shares when prices are high. Instead of worrying about timing the market (buying low, selling high), you achieve a reasonable average cost per share. You also benefit from compounding because you're not waiting to invest by 'timing the market'. With the power of compounding and time on your side, you can greatly benefit from this method.

Pay Less Tax, Get Richer Quicker

HERE'S ANOTHER BIT of knowledge that we hope you will store away for a day down the road when it will become extremely useful. We know that retirement is a long way off but this is way too important for you not to know.

THERE ARE FINANCIAL vehicles set up that encourage you to save for your retirement. They are known variously as Individual Retirement Accounts (IRAs) or Retirement Savings Plans (RRSPs). They amount to the same thing. Encouraging you to save for your retirement will take the pressure off future governments, so they allow you to make money within a savings plan without having to pay any taxes on the gains...for a while.

WHEN YOU OPEN an account and make a contribution, depending on local laws, that amount may be deductible against your taxes. Inside the plan, you invest in any of the traditional options: Stocks, mutual funds, CDs etc., but as opposed to investments made outside a plan, any profits, dividends or gains you make are not subject to taxation. Over the years of contributing—the longer the better—you gain from compounding without losing any part of it to taxes. When you retire, you should have a substantial nest-egg on which to draw. In some, not all jurisidications, when you start to take money out of the plan it will be treated as income and you will pay tax.

We HAVE to believe in ourselves

COMPARISON of an IRA VS a NON-TAX SHELTERED SAVINGS INVESTMENT.

Each person deposits $4,000 per year at an interest rate of 12%. Both are in the 40% tax bracket.

	Person A Not Tax Sheltered	Person B ROTH IRA
Value at year 10	67,824	74, 678
Value at year 20	195,744	306,616
Value at year 30	452,123	1,026,981
Value at year 40	965,966	3,264,324

Explanation of Above Chart

THE CASE OF Person A illustrates the limited wealth accumulation in a non-sheltered savings investment. Because they are paying taxes on all their profits, a 12 per cent yield (profit) to someone in the 40 per cent tax bracket would effectively leave the person with a 7.2 per cent profit. After 40 years of investing the total will only be $965,966. Not that this is an insignificant amount. And, it is certainly far greater than what the average person has to retire on. But, look at person B. **By investing the same amount of money in a retirement plan he or she would have accumulated over three million dollars! A $2,298,358 bonus.** That's because they are not paying any taxes on their yearly profits, so all the profits are continually being reinvested.

A RETIREMENT PLAN is a very important aspect of wealth building that almost everyone

can take advantage of. Local laws vary widely on contribution ceilings and options so we encourage you to research this area. For most young people in the U.S. a ROTH IRA is an unbeatable investment in the future.

Investing in Yourself

EACH OF US has the ability to succeed at what we really love but the first step along the journey is we have to believe in ourselves and our abilities. As simple as it sounds it can be the difference between success and failure. Everyone has incredible possibilities available to them. We have to learn to see them, and act on them. And that means education.

We have to believe in ourselves and our abilities.

IN NORTH AMERICA over the next 20 years, it is estimated that more than 75% of all jobs will require a college education, and that fewer than 6% of new jobs will need workers with only a high school education. Over the past 20 years thousands of North American jobs have vanished. Factories have gone silent and towns have died. Those jobs have

been shipped to countries like China and India where weekly wages are appallingly low. We can, as a result, buy MP3 players and CD burners for $50. But you should not be concerned about those jobs, they're not much fun and they're not for you because you live in North America. **If you take advantage of the North American education system you can move way beyond those kinds of jobs** to creative, interesting work which pays way better and is much more fun. As awful as school can seem some days, an education is simply the way— pretty much the only way now— to expand your opportunities in a limitless way. Now, we've all heard stories about people who

have become incredibly rich with very little formal education. It happens. The important thing to remember is that these people are the exceptions, not the rule. Your dreams, if they're big enough, will require as much education as you can get before you start to build them. Pity the dropout; they are placing huge limits on their future even before they get started.

WHETHER OR NOT you complete a college education, **we believe in life-long learning**. This means identifying and embracing bold new ideas, continuous investment in yourself through reading, listening to books on CD, taking courses, receiving coaching from mentors and through learning by doing.

10 Ways to PAY for COLLEGE

Student Loan debt **exceeds** $60 Billion dollars.

1. **Get as much information as you can before you turn 15. Your high school guidance office is a great place to start. There you will find:**
   - **College programs and admissions requirements**
   - **Required high school courses**
   - **Available grants, scholarships**
   - **Loan options**

2. **You can apply for a Stafford Loan, a government loan available to everyone without regard for family income.**

3. **Apply for a Pell Grant of up to $ 3,000 per school year if your parent's income is below a certain level.**

4. **Consider a college in your own community, as you may be able to stay at home for little or no room & board fees.**

5. **Obtain an associate's degree by getting a 2-year degree and then transferring for full credit to a 4-year program. This can save you about 40% in total costs.**

6. **Join the Armed Forces and obtain a "free" college education.**

7. **Work at the college and receive both your paycheck and a staff discount on tuition.**

8. **Work for a company that sponsors continuing education and refunds part or all of your tuition.**

9. **Join a work-study program that pays your way through college while gaining valuable on-the-job experience.**

10. **Some private colleges allow you to pre-pay your tuition at any age. If you don't end up attending that school you get your money back. Since tuition is slated to increase each year, you can pay for school in 2010 at today's rates.**

Photo courtesy of Subway®

FRED DELUCA

Teen Just Wants to Pay for College

IT WAS THE summer of 1965, in Bridgeport, Connecticut. 17-year-old high school graduate, Fred DeLuca was looking for a way to make enough money to pay for his University tuition. The solution came at a backyard barbecue during a conversation with family friend, Dr. Peter Buck. He suggested that Fred open a submarine sandwich shop after having seen a similar sandwich shop in his hometown experience huge success. Fred states, **"that the suggestion to open a sandwich shop was the best advice he has ever received."**

WITH A $1,000 loan from the doctor, a partnership was formed and Pete's Super Submarines opened in August. Their second location opened a year later and Fred quickly realized that marketing and visibility were going to be key factors in the success of the business. His third store was in a highly visible location and it's still serving sandwiches today. Fred attributes his success to "Persistence. It's key... and the willingness to find new ways to accomplish your objectives." The name was shortened from Pete's Super Submarines to Subway® at that time. Subway® was recognized as the #1 franchise on the Franchise 500 list of 2005. In 2005 the SUBWAY® chain entered its 40th year of operation. It is the world's largest submarine sandwich chain with more than 23,000 restaurants in 80 countries. As a matter of fact, the SUBWAY® chain operates more units in the US and Canada than McDonald's®. **Not bad for a seventeen-year-old kid from "the projects" who just needed to earn his tuition.**

> **"Don't worry how big the business you start is, just be sure to get started. If you start small early in life there's a good chance of Finishing Big."**
> — Fred DeLuca

Photo courtesy of Subway®

SO FAR, WE'VE covered the critical importance of your Attitude to making money and we've reviewed the critical Behaviors. **The final step is intended for those who want to really accelerate their income by becoming their own boss.** Just before that step, let's review what you've learned in this chapter.

IN THIS CHAPTER

In this chapter you should have learned some of the Behaviors for saving the money you worked so hard to earn as well as some strategies to put that money to work for you. The key is to take action. If you find yourself wasting money on things you don't really need, stop. If you want to get money without having to do any work, start a savings plan now. Investing as little as $5 every week will have a big impact over time. The hardest part is taking the first step and that really isn't hard at all. Trust us, when you look back, you will be REALLY glad you started today!

1 **What does Frugality mean to you?**

2 **What is the Money Snapshot, and how should it be used?**

3 **What are some of the most common rip-offs?**

4 **Who is your Financial "Bud"?**

5 **What are the three different types of leveraging, and which one holds the most interest to you?**

6 **What did you learn about yourself as a result of completing the Employability Quiz?**

7 **What is the "Rule of 72" and how will mastering this principle change your life?**

8 **What is the most effective way to use credit cards?**

9 **What is life insurance for? What is it not for? What is the best type of life insurance?**

10 **What is the best investment type, and why?**

Creation of Money

now we get to the really fun section of the book. This is where you get to let your imagination run wild and follow the ideas that thrill you the most. The fact is that three-quarters of all self-made millionaires own one or more businesses. The attractions are pretty clear: you will make more money and you will take control of your own life. It's true that the added risk will require a stronger stomach and that kind of uncertainty is not for everybody. That's OK. If you integrate into your life even a few of the ideas and Behaviors you found in the first two sections of this book, you'll be much further ahead. And, you can always try out some ideas on a part-time basis while you are still in school, or later if you have a full-time job.

ISN'T THIS WORTH SAVING?

At the age of 12 he started to grow concerned when he saw images of hurricanes on the east coast and earthquakes and fires in the west. Then he saw a story

Together they lobbied major retailers to stop using fur in their clothing.

IN THE MANY years we've been working with self-made millionaires and successful entrepreneurs, we've noticed one trait common to them all: **Passion**. This is what gets them through the rough times and sets their products and services apart from the competition. When you're passionate about a project, it no longer seems like 'work' and the hours invested seem to melt away.

Danny Seo HAS a passion. It's for the future of the planet, and along the way it's made him rich.

about the inhumane treatment of chickens on a factory farm. It affected him so much that the next day, which just happened to be Earth Day and his birthday, he

gathered his friends together and formed 'Earth 2000' dedicated to saving the planet. **His small group of friends grew from 6 to an organization of 20,000** across the country, all dedicated to doing the right thing for the future. Together they lobbied politicians, planned boycotts and convinced major retailers such as Eddie Bauer and Lerner New York to stop using fur in their clothing.

> **"Whoever wants to be great must become a servant."**
> — Mark 10:43

ALONG THE WAY Danny learned the value of organizing people and the power of public relations. At age 18 he turned his experiences with the group he founded into a deal with Ballantine Books. Billed as 'activism for beginners' **"Generation React" earned Danny a $33,000 advance.** These days Danny is preparing the launch of a range of eco-friendly products. Danny says that sales of green and cruelty free products exceed a staggering $100 billion every year. He's about to go into production on his own television show that will combine education and planet awareness with sales of his products.

HIS THIRD BOOK "Conscious Style Home" continues to underline his belief that anyone can make a difference if they want to. He says **"People who are going to be successful should have passion and desire in their hearts for whatever they're working toward."** Now based in New York, he is in constant demand as a speaker and for interviews in magazines like "People" and on TV programs such as Oprah. Making a difference has made a huge difference in the lives of the many people Danny has affected and profoundly changed his economic life in the process. ◘

Photo courtesy of Lauren Hefferon

TOURING THROUGH TUSCANY

Classic Adventures

EVER SINCE HIGH school **Lauren Hefferon** has been passionate about cycling. She also loved to travel. For her the obvious answer was to combine the two. After experiencing several Outward Bound courses she decided to work as a bike tour guide during her college years. In 1988 she combined all her passions (cycling, visual arts, outdoor education and her family's Italian roots) by starting up Ciclismo Classico, an adventure travel company that organizes bike tours throughout Italy, New England, France, Spain and Ireland. Cycling and travel are now both her passion and her profit. She enjoys a comfortable lifestyle and the company of like-minded people.

WHEN SHE SPEAKS to other young entrepreneurs, she leaves them with the image of the all-important sail in sail boating. She says, **"Your passion for your business is like the wind. It gives you momentum, however, without the appropriate skills and knowledge of using the sail you won't get anywhere."** She goes on to encourage business owners to invest in themselves by taking business courses, reading books and tapping into the power of a mentor. The business has been growing steadily. Currently she employs 20 tour guides and 10 support staff. Her average tour group size is 14, and to date over 5,000 clients have enjoyed tours with the company.

Travelling and cycling... the obvious answer was to combine the two.

ELISE AND EVAN MACMILLAN

Making a Million Bucks...Sweet!

MAKING A MILLION dollars doesn't need to be a complicated exercise. **Elise Macmillan** began making chocolate candy with her grandmother at age 3 because she loved it. A few years ago, at age 13, she started selling her chocolate creations, **Brown Cows, Pigs in Mud and Pecan Turtles** in her Denver community. Elise says her motivation to start the business was, "to gain a sense of personal control over what we were doing. Looking back, I would say it was a feeling of empowerment."

SHE WAS SO successful that she formed a company called The Chocolate Farm and, with her brother, **Evan**, built a website (WWW.THECHOCOLATEFARM.COM) to expand their sales base. It worked. They now have 40 employees, their products are sold on 5 continents and they enjoy sales in excess of $1 million!

"THE SINGLE BIGGEST key to our success is that we have a great story. People can relate to it, and the media loves it. In fact the business really started because we had to find a way to fulfill all of the orders caused by the media attention."

EVAN HAS THIS advice for teens who want to try their own ideas: "Take risks while you're young. Don't just think about it, get into action and do it now! Read tons of stuff about current events; know what's going on around you and how it affects you, read trade journals and business magazines." He also recommends reading about and, whenever possible, meeting "....Real entrepreneurs who despite their fears and obstacles take the risks to follow their dreams."

ELISE AND EVAN Macmillan received an Ernst & Young Entrepreneur of the Year Award in 1999 and have been featured in PEOPLE Magazine, the Wall Street Journal and Teen Magazine. They've appeared on Oprah, The Early Show on CBS, FoodTV, CNN and on Fox National News. They've turned a 'sweet tooth' into a very sweet life.

AFTER READING THE preceeding stories you may be thinking the business idea that's been brewing in your head just might work. If you have a business idea, further on in this chapter we will show you a way to test it to increase your odds of success. If you don't currently have any one business idea in mind, but are intrigued with the prospect of starting your own business, the following section provides a list of business ideas to consider.

It was a feeling of empowerment.

10 BUSINESS Ideas Around the House

☞ **Babysitting/Parent's helper**

☞ **House and garage cleaning**

☞ **Yard work – mowing grass, raking leaves, trimming bushes, raking leaves, snow removal**

☞ **House sitter**

☞ **Painting /small household repairs**

☞ **Pet care/pet walking**

☞ **Weekly car washing/cleaning**

☞ **Home pool care**

☞ **Laundry service/pickup & delivery**

☞ **Organization of various collections/books, CDs, DVD/ videos**

Other great ideas that come to mind:

_____

_____

_____

Bringing Home the Bacon

Photo courtesy of Abbey Fleck

ABBEY FLECK

MINNESOTA'S Abbey Fleck was 8 years old when she had her 'eureka' moment. She was cooking bacon with her dad, Jon, one Saturday morning. When they ran out of paper towels to soak up the grease they improvised by using a newspaper. Mom was not impressed. If only there was something they could use so that the grease dripped into a dish. Necessity being the 'Mother' of invention, they started experimenting. **"We made a few prototypes which seemed to** work, then we started questioning whether there was a market for something like it. Without giving the idea away we started asking everybody what they disliked most about bacon. Everyone said the same thing, that it was 'too messy' and that if there was a way of eliminating the mess, they would be interested. As a bonus, the bacon is MUCH healthier by cooking it this way."

WITH THIS CRUDE but effective market research in hand they started to explore the costs of manufacturing her invention. To be successful they knew it would have to be very high quality yet inexpensive. They spoke to a number of successful entrepreneurs who offered very good advice, and then they took the risk.

People loved the fact that this device was designed by an 8 year old.

"ONCE WE FOUND the right mould for manufacture we had to buy huge amounts of plastic to make it worthwhile. My grandfather helped us out by taking a mortgage on his farm. Once we did the first run, it just built from

there. We got lots of free publicity because we had a good story. People loved the fact that this device was designed by an 8 year old. That got them interested. When they found out it was also a good product, everyone wanted one."

SINCE THEN THEY'VE sold millions, keeping manufacturing plants busy 24 hours a day, 7 days a week. Their success has allowed her family to enjoy a great lifestyle. Her mother, brothers and sisters were all able to complete college and travel, and Abbey herself is now enjoying life at UCLA. Her advice for other young inventors: "When you're 8, every idea seems like a great one. You really need the help of a parent to decide whether the idea already exists and if it's actually marketable. **The best ideas come when you're just going through your day and stumble across one.** When you try and force an idea it doesn't really work."

10 BUSINESS Ideas Providing Personal Services

☞ **School tutoring**

☞ **Planning Kid Parties/Magic or puppet shows/clown**

☞ **Dance organizer/DJ**

☞ **Personal Trainer/One on One Coach**

☞ **Musician or music tutor**

☞ **Reading for seniors or blind people**

☞ **Moving people locally**

☞ **Gift shopping and wrapping**

☞ **Grocery shopping**

☞ **Running errands for seniors**

Other great ideas that come to mind:

_____

_____

_____

Photo courtesy of Aaron Shaughnessy

TENNIS FOR SUCCESS

Tennis Anyone?

Aaron Shaughnessy, a full-time university student, needed money for tuition. He was a good tennis player, and had a talent for teaching others how to play, so a summer job as a tennis instructor was a natural first step. Aaron describes it as "A great job, fantastic kids to work with; lousy pay!" He earned only about $1,700 per summer. Aaron decided to take charge of his situation and convinced his home town to put him in charge of its entire summer tennis program. He hired 3 friends as instructors, paid them better than elsewhere and offered tennis camps throughout the summer at four locations he rented from the city. **That summer he made $30,000 profit and has made plans to expand his business.**

Photo courtesy of Shazad Mohamed

SHAZAD MOHAMED

ALMOST EVERYONE GROWS up with some daily exposure to computers. They're a great tool for research, for fun and, most importantly for our purposes here, for starting up your own business. Shazad Mohamed started exploring this "mysterious device" at age 3. "With the computer and the internet there are so many levels involved. The more I learned the more I realized that I didn't know enough and the more I wanted to explore."

SHAZAD WAS EQUALLY interested in how businesses worked and by age 12 was ready to set up his company, http://www.globaltek-solutions.com an e-business solutions provider. He says he simply saw a great opportunity and went for it. Six years later, at age 18,

he has a multi-million-dollar business employing 50 people around the world.

"WHEN I WAS starting up the business I had the full support of my parents. They gave me good feedback. As well, I looked at several local successful entrepreneurs and went after them. If you surround yourself with great people, you're much better off. Relationships are key. You can do great things with great people around you."

DEVELOPING MENTORS CAN be hugely rewarding, especially when starting up a business. "Getting Venture Capital money when you're 12 years old is very difficult. I had to think of very creative ways of starting the busi-

10 BUSINESS Ideas
Using Technology

☞ **Creating Web-sites**

☞ **Data-base management and targeted email marketing**

☞ **Word Processing**

☞ **Desktop Publishing – Designing business cards, brochures, signs, flyers, menus.**

☞ **Computer services: maintenance, virus protection, weekly data back-ups, network set-up & management**

☞ **Computer programming/ software development**

☞ **Teaching computer skills to seniors.**

☞ **Transferring home videos/slides to DVD**

☞ **Computer purchasing consultant**

☞ **Beta-testing (Soft-ware, games, hardware)**

Other great ideas that come to mind:

_____

_____

ness. I focused my efforts on consulting and developing software for the customer's needs and built up the capital base from there."

"IT'S IMPORTANT TO be passionate about your idea. If you look at it as a hobby it will be easier because then it's not work. Be creative; leverage all the tools around you and find mentors to help you."

"I'M REALLY EXCITED about the future. There is much, much, much more to do!"

Delivering the Goods

IN 1907, SEATTLE teen entrepreneur **Jim Casey** borrowed $100 to begin American Messenger Co. Competition was fierce and Jim and his partners felt they needed an edge. So, they committed themselves to a simple slogan: best service—lowest rates. They backed the slogan up by offering the first reliable round-the-clock service by uniformed couriers. This humble bicycle messenger service grew up to become UPS, one of the world's largest global transportation companies.

10 BUSINESS Ideas
Serving Other Businesses

☞ **Commercial property management – lawn, gardens & parking lot**

☞ **Office helper & odd jobs**

☞ **Trash and recycling removal, plant care**

☞ **Envelope addressing/ stuffing and bulk mailing**

☞ **Photography (products, personnel, business location)**

☞ **Organization of files, warehouse inventory**

☞ **Local delivery/ courier service**

☞ **Research and report generation service**

☞ **Mobile vendor: coffee, tea, soda, juice, snacks**

☞ **Flyer and advertising brochure distribution**

Other great ideas that come to mind:

_____

_____

Best Service Lowest Rates

Photo courtesy of Carlee & Christy

CARLEE & CHRISTY PANYLYK

The Information Highway is Paved With Gold

16 year old **Matthew Lee's** total business start up cost was $1,500 and 90% of that was in equipment that he personally wanted to own, such as a professional digital camera. Matthew likes collectables. His hobby is to go to wholesalers, flea markets, garage sales and auctions where, with his keen eye for value, he would purchase items at very low prices and re-sell to local people. It occurred to him that he could turn this into a business using the Internet. Now he auctions off his inventory to the highest bidder through EBay.

USING THE BASIC computer in his house he has created a thriving business with over 90% of its sales from overseas. He maintains a minimum markup of 3 times. So, for example if he pays 1 dollar for something he sells it within one week for at least 3 dol-

Youth Entrepreneurship is in Fashion

Young entrepreneurs **Carlee & Christy Panylyk** have been in business for themselves since they were nine and six years of age respectively. C & C Creations is a multi-award winning business making beaded and pewter necklaces. Sold at 300 retail outlets from coast-to-coast, sales have topped $800,000. At peak production, assemblers were making 8,000 necklaces a month to keep up with the demand. The sisters employed their mother full-time for five years and hired their high school principal as a Sales Representative. His wife became an assembler.

CARLEE AND CHRISTY'S advice to young entrepreneurs is to find "a mentor to support them in decision making & strategic plan-

ning. Guidance from an adult can make a world of difference when it comes to the success of your business." They also believe, **"If you have passion then the work does not seem tedious. If it's not fun, don't do it!".**

A whole other category of business ideas involve simply buying something in one place and selling it somewhere else at a higher price. The possibilities here are almost endless:

1 **Find discounted and under-priced goods and resell them at a profit.**

2 **Add value to an existing item, for instance, fixing a beat-up bicycle or restoring old furniture.**

3 **Combining, which means buying several items in, for example, a dollar store, putting them together to make what can now be sold as a gift basket worth more than the price of the goods inside. In the same way, take some beads, some threads, clasps and instructions, now you have a hobby kit.**

Other great ideas that come to mind:

_____

_____

lars. He routinely sells products for much higher profits such as the WWI British Military Candy Box. He invested $20 to buy it and sold it for $120. He purchased an 1885 war medal for $50.00 and was able to quickly sell it online for $600.00! Matthew says his key to success is, "first of all I enjoy collectables, so it never feels like work to me.

THE FACT THAT I can earn a couple of thousand dollars a week, part-time, doing something that I love is very cool!"

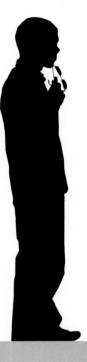

Doing something that I LOVE is very Cool.

10 BUSINESS Ideas
Making Stuff

☞ **Design personalized greeting cards, T-Shirts with special design or photos**

☞ **Make jewelry**

☞ **Grow and sell garden vegetables and fruit**

☞ **Make kid's lunches**

☞ **Make gift baskets - special event or seasonal**

☞ **Lemonade / Slushy / Popcorn / Candy Apple Stand**

☞ **Making Crafts – Candles, toys, Christmas ornaments, bird feeders, CD Stands, custom kites, potted plants**

☞ **Clothes/ Accessories, Hats, scarves, belts**

☞ **Temporary henna tattoos or face painting**

☞ **Make costumes/ Halloween/ special events/ kids playtime**

Other great ideas that come to mind:

_____

_____

Photo courtesy of Gina Gallant

GINA GALLANT

Take What You're Passionate About and Turn it into a Business

AS WE'VE SAID earlier, many of the best businesses have started because the person was passionate about some product or service. That passion gets conveyed to the customer, suppliers and co-workers, and it creates a great environment for success. It also makes the long hours of work easier to accept.

Recycled Success

THEY SAY THE road to success always has some rough spots, so why not smooth them out with recycled plastic? That's the idea from **Gina Gallant** of Prince George, British Columbia. When she was 13 she got the idea to mix recyclable plastic bottles with crushed stone and asphalt. "You see, asphalt and plastic are both derived from hydrocarbons and therefore compatible." The mixture saves the plastic from going to landfill and makes the road surface quieter to drive on.

GINA, WHO IS now 18, says, "It took me a couple of years to develop. First I ground the plastic in our home blender. That was really loud! Then I mixed in some aggregate which is what they use on roads. It took a while to get the mixture right but even longer to convince people to take me seriously. Initially they thought I was too young and because I'm a girl, they just didn't listen. It took a lot of personal strength to continue but because I believed so strongly in what I was doing, I eventually convinced the town to let me try my idea."

"THEY GAVE ME a stretch of road for the experiment as long as I worked with a regular paving company. So, I had to convince them that being a girl and young was not a negative. Finally I became project coordinator at age 15."

I GUESS I always had some self-doubt and that made it more difficult because everyone was saying I couldn't do it. I think if you really believe in what you're doing and you really want to help people you'll overcome the objections because your passion is stronger than your doubts."

GINA'S OTHER INVENTION is a bike helmet that glows when it is worn correctly. It's fun for kids, it's safe, and wearing it properly makes it easier for drivers to see the young cyclists. "My little brother was hit by a car when he was 5 and he would have died if he wasn't wearing a helmet. Lots of people don't wear helmets and that's just crazy! I'd love to change that thinking."

> **First I ground the plastic in our home blender. That was really LOUD.**

"THERE'S NOTHING YOU can't do if you believe in yourself. Believe in yourself and follow your heart. If you convince yourself, then everyone else will follow. I really like helping people, and I love science. Making money from inventions is just a bonus." ⦿

The Right Note

Setting up a new business doesn't have to mean reaching far beyond your own experiences. Ask yourself what you love to do or what you're naturally good at. **Nicholas Ravagni** started playing guitar when he was 5 and never stopped. He says music "can bring you up when you're feeling down and get you through the bad times."

PLAYING COMES NATURALLY for Nicholas. At age 6 he invented a system that, he says, will teach anyone how to play guitar **(HTTP://WWW.DONTFRET.COM)**. **Receiving a patent for his device at age 10 made him one of the youngest patent-holders** in America. Shortly thereafter Hal Leonard, the world's largest printed music retailer, began distributing his invention.

NICHOLAS SAYS "IF you have a really good idea, go for it! Don't take 'No' for an answer. Check first to make sure no one else has already made your product. Then thoroughly research the company you'll be doing business with, whether it's a manufacturer or a distributor, and have a lawyer review all contracts before you sign them."

"AT FIRST I had the usual problem that teens have when trying

Photo courtesy of Nicholas Ravagni

NICHOLAS RAVAGNI

to set up a business, but when they heard the pitch, saw the research I'd done, the written material and the patent, they knew I was serious. It all goes back to 'don't take 'No' for an answer.'"

NICHOLAS HAS RECEIVED more patents, one for an adaptation of his invention for violin **(HTTP://WWW.FRETLESSFINGER-GUIDES.COM)** and another for an electronic version that will guide guitar player's fingers to the right positions via light emitting polymers hooked up to a computer. If you have an idea worth patenting Nicholas recommends checking out the U.S. patent office http://www.uspto.gov for some useful tools and a great search function.

"BE PASSIONATE IN the pursuit of your dreams and you will find true harmony in the rhythms of your life." ⦿

Make your life easier ...then get rich.

SOMETIMES, SOMETHING YOU create to save yourself some work or to make your life easier is just the thing that other people need as well. Remember the Makin' Bacon idea? Solving other people's challenges can make you rich.

EVER EATEN A PowerBar for a snack? If you choose the ones without all the sugar and fat they can be a great snack without adding the pounds to your waistline. This clever idea didn't come out of a multinational's kitchen, it was the brainchild of former marathoner **Brian Maxwell**. Always on the look for an easy to carry, nutritious energy boost while running, he developed the PowerBar in his kitchen and began selling them to friends and clients out of his living room in 1986. Fourteen years later he and his wife, Jennifer, sold their Berkley, California based company to Nestle for $375 million. ⦿

AFTER READING ABOUT other teens who have taken the entrepreneurial challenge, you may want to take the next few self-assessment tests to evaluate your own tendencies.

The ABCs of Making Money 4 Teens
Entrepeneurial Indicator

Instructions: Circle the number that comes closest to representing how true the statement is for you right now (a rating of 1 would represent never true, while a rating of 5 would represent always true).

PART ONE: Entrepreneurial Characteristics Statements   **Rating**

Statement					
I believe that taking reasonable risks is what life is all about.	1	2	3	4	5
I always strive to be the best, faster or the first at whatever I do.	1	2	3	4	5
I want to be successful so much it dominates my daily thoughts.	1	2	3	4	5
I believe that for me, failure is not an option.	1	2	3	4	5
I double my efforts to respond to setbacks.	1	2	3	4	5
I often get so focused on my projects that I forget everything else.	1	2	3	4	5
I believe that despite any obstacles I will succeed.	1	2	3	4	5
I respond well under situations of pressure and stress.	1	2	3	4	5
I can stabilize a situation by reducing the risks.	1	2	3	4	5
I am seen by others as adventurous, ambitious, energetic and optimistic.	1	2	3	4	5

Interpretation: A score of 40 or higher demonstrates strong Attitudes that can serve you very well on your entrepreneurial journey. A lower score indicates that you need to do some more thinking about what you want to do. Maybe it would be better to work on your idea with someone who is more comfortable with the risks of having their own business. There's nothing wrong with being 'the idea person' for someone else, or for a company. Just try to keep as much ownership and control of the idea as possible.

The ABCs of Making Money 4 Teens
Entrepeneurial Indicator

PART TWO: A Partial List of Entrepreneurial Skills

As a potential business owner, you should know something about every aspect of it. Try this self-assessment exercise to measure your entrepreneurial skills. When you're done, use the "No's" and "Uncertain's" to highlight those things you need to work on. The more of these skills you have, the greater the chance your business idea will blossom into something real. If you lack any of these skills you can upgrade them by reading, by learning from someone who has already done what you're trying to do, by taking on a knowledgeable partner or a new employee skilled in that area, or by handing the job over to outsiders with the right skills.

Entrepreneurial Skill.	Yes	No	Uncertain	Area to Improve
Buying stuff at low price	——	——	——	——
Making stuff	——	——	——	——
Organizing	——	——	——	——
Quality Control	——	——	——	——
Problem Solving	——	——	——	——
Decision Making	——	——	——	——
Leading People	——	——	——	——
Using Computers	——	——	——	——
Bookkeeping & Budgeting	——	——	——	——
Keeping Costs Low	——	——	——	——
Understanding Customer's Wants	——	——	——	——
Selling Stuff at a Profit	——	——	——	——
Providing Quality Customer Service	——	——	——	——
Advertising/Creative promotions	——	——	——	——

My Entrepeneurial Style

Instructions: Please review the four words in row 1 going across the page. Ask yourself, which of the four words in row 1 is most like you; in the space just to the right of the word write the number "4." Then review the three remaining words in row 1. Now ask yourself which of the remaining words is most like you, place the number "3" to the right of that word. Repeat the same instructions filling in the numbers "2" and "1" to the right of the appropriate words. Please note you can only have one 4, one 3, one 2, and one 1 per each row. Upon completion every word must have a number to the right of it.

1 Dominating	Sensitive	Easy-going	Outspoken
2 Inventive	Accurate	Sincere	Outgoing
3 Inflexible	Cautious	Indecisive	Erratic
4 Confident	Traditional	Likeable	Playful
5 Productive	Structured	Helpful	Creative
6 Controlling	Suspicious	Naïve	Impulsive
7 Overbearing	Rigid	Shy	Unorganized
8 Guarded	Perfectionist	Stubborn	Exact
Subtotal B	**Subtotal O**	**Subtotal G**	**Subtotal P**

Scoring: Once you have completed the above exercise, please take a moment and add each of the four columns to obtain four subtotals. One final task is to add up the four subtotals, this grand total number must equal 80. If it does not equal 80 please review your addition.

Interpretation: Review your four subtotals; the subtotal with the highest number reflects your dominant Entrepreneur Style. Take note of the single letter to the right of each subtotal. That letter corresponds to one of the four styles on the next page. If, for example your highest column is the first, your Entrepreneur Style is the "B" or Bull Style. If your highest subtotals are tied, it means that your Entrepreneur Style is influenced by several styles. Once you have read your style ask yourself the following questions:

- **What do you think about your results?**

- **Have you learned anything new about yourself?**

- **Do any business ideas come to mind that would be ideally suited to your Entrepreneur Style?**

Understanding My Entrepreneurial Style

PEACOCK

Showy and Creative Entertainer

- Creative and entertaining
- Decides quickly and spontaneously
- High need for socializing and fun
- Wants approval and recognition
- Seeks freedom to express self
- Fast starters, entertainers and effective persuaders
- Dislikes details
- Resists regulation, routine & perfectionism

Possible business ideas: fashion design, entertainer, party planner, inventor

GOLDEN LAB

Loyal and Helpful Friend

- Caring, very people oriented
- Risk and stress avoider
- Cautious decision maker/dislikes impatience & being rushed
- Relationships/communication is important
- Wants to be included and accepted by others
- Unstructured, creative, and relaxed
- Fears unexpected situations and change

Possible business ideas: parent helper, tutor, sports instructor

BULL

Action and Focused Doer

- Results and goal driven
- Decides quickly and conclusively
- Acts fast in a definite way
- Secure when in charge of situation/ fears loss of control
- Impatient/insensitive and dislikes details
- Assesses others by their performance, results & success record
- Inspired with winning

Possible business ideas: sales broker, Personal trainer, fundraiser

OWL

Wise and Cautious Thinker

- Logical and controlling
- Cautious decision maker/decision based on research
- Wants facts, details and accuracy
- Acts slowly and systematically
- Structured, practical and formal
- Dislikes impatience, being rushed or disorganization
- Tends to procrastinate, be critical, resists delegation

Possible business ideas: computer programmer, personal organizer, clipping service

Turning Your Hobbies into Wealth

PROSPECTIVE ENTREPRENEURS OFTEN make the mistake of narrowing their choices too quickly; starting with the first business that comes to mind. Use the following guide to try to expand your choices and come up with ideas for businesses that you would actually enjoy running. The object is to discover those business opportunities that are not only profitable but also personally rewarding. The trick is to match the business to your preferences, rather than vice versa.

HERE ARE A few quick steps to start you off:

Money Making Ideas – Quick Assessment

STEP 1. Write down all your interests, hobbies, leisure activities, and the previous work or volunteer experiences that you have enjoyed. For example: music, working with animals, cooking, shopping, organizing events or developing web sites.

_____

_____

STEP 2. The next step is to convert your interest into money-making opportunities. For example, if you like working with children and playing musical instruments, you might want to be a performer at kid's parties or be a music tutor. Or, if you are interested in photography and enjoy meeting people, perhaps a videotaping service would be right for you.

_____

_____

STEP 3. Now, narrow the list down to the three or four money making business ideas that appeal to you the most.

_____

_____

STEP 4. Analyze each of the above money-making ideas by answering the following questions:

_____

_____

- **What is the product and or service you will offer?**
- **Will you produce or purchase this product?**
- **Who will buy it? How big is the potential market?**
- **What problems or opportunities will your product or service address?**
- **What price should you charge?**
- **What costs do you have to deal with?**
- **Who is your competition? What strengths do they have over you and your business idea?**
- **What advantages do you have over the competition?**
- **How much money do you plan to generate with this business idea?**
- **How much time, energy and effort will it take to create a successful business?**
- **Whose help will you require to become successful?**
- **How much start-up money will you require?**
- **Can you secure the necessary start-up funds? How?**
- **What production tools/facilities are required?**
- **What permits/licenses are required prior to start-up?**
- **What raw goods/supplies will you require?**
- **What are the potential risks associated with this idea?**
- **What other information do you require prior to starting?**

The ABCs of Making Money 4 Teens
Business Start-up Planner

Upfront Costs	Total
Business Idea Research costs	
Permits/Licenses	
P.O. Box Rental	
Telephone/ Cell Phone	
Internet	
Marketing Material (Business cards, flyers, signs etc)	
Business Supplies	
Purchase /Rent equipment	
Professional fees (Bookkeeper, Legal, Consulting)	
Facility Rental	
Other	
Total Up-Front Costs	
Total Available Start-Up Capital	
Shortage or Surplus of Start-Up Capital	
Ongoing Monthly Business Costs	
Rental facility/equipment	
Telephone	
Cost to purchase or produce goods for resale	
Local travel	
Postage	
Sales Commissions	
Out-Sourcing Fees	
Employee Wages	
Other	
Total Monthly Business Costs	
Projected Monthly Sales	
Net Difference	

Reviewing the Results:

For every question you answered "I Don't Know", you will have to do further research. Consider making some basic changes to improve your idea and then test it again. If it still doesn't look promising, file the idea and move on to test a different one.

STEP 5: Reality Check

After completing step 4, share your analysis of your business idea with several trusted people with business experience. They may see pitfalls or opportunities that you don't.

7 STEPS to
Business Start-up

1   Select a business idea that you are passionate about and fulfills the criteria in the Analysis and Realty Check steps you've just completed.

2   Determine a business structure (Sole Proprietorship, Partnership or Incorporated Company). Check out www.deptofcommerce.org for more info.

3   Come up with a catchy business name and a logo (Check out some of the free clip art galleries found on-line) Create promotional material with your logo and contact information on it.

4   Secure suppliers for raw materials, obtain necessary equipment, produce goods.

5   Have the following supplies: Order form, receipt book, business cards, calendar/day book/PDA to track appointments and jobs, address book/PDA to keep customer information, invoices, income and expense tracker.

6   Open a bank account.

7   Go get customers!

Remember Safety First! Consider the following risks:

Personal safety (equipment – power tools, ladders etc.)

Personal information: telephone number, home and email address etc. Consider getting a separate phone line, postal box etc. Make sure meetings are held in a safe location.

Employee safety: same advice as above, remember as an employer you have legal obligations for the safety of your staff

Legal issues: be aware of the laws and regulations that pertain to your business.

Financial issues: as the business owner you need to be aware of all the financial risks prior to starting any business. You may be personally responsible for covering any losses!

ALWAYS REVIEW THESE ISSUES WITH A
TRUSTED, KNOWLEDGEABLE ADULT!!!

LOOKING FOR MORE HELP?

THE NATIONAL FOUNDATION FOR TEACHING ENTREPRENEURSHIP. (NFTE)

Remember Migdalia Morales? She's the one who escaped the projects of Massachusetts to start several successful businesses. The organization that helped her has helped over 100,000 other teenagers across America and around the world. It was started in 1987 by Steve Mariotti, a high school teacher from New York's tough South Bronx area. Steve's background as a business executive and entrepreneur helped inspire kids who were at risk for dropping out of school and repeating the pattern of poverty from which they came.

Steve believes that "When low-income youth are given the opportunity to learn about entrepreneurship, their innate 'street smarts' can easily develop into 'academic smarts' and 'business smarts'."

Specializing in teens from low-income communities NFTE trains teachers to deliver the NFTE curriculum through NFTE University and calls them Certified Entrepreneurship Teachers (CETs). Most CETs are public school teachers, although they also have trained some business people and NFTE alumni to be CETs. Their mission is to teach the essentials in getting a business off the ground from planning to full development of the idea. Check out their website for more information at: HTTP://WWW.NFTE.COM

JUNIOR ACHIEVEMENT (JA)

This is another great organization dedicated to teaching young people the principles of business. They have branches throughout North America, in fact there are chapters in many schools. They organize local and State competitions for young entrepreneurs which is a great way to get you and your ideas noticed. It's also a great addition to any resume. Check out WWW.JA.ORG

45 East Clubhouse Dr. Colorado Springs, CO. 80906
719-540-8000.

Canada: 1 Westside Dr. Toronto, Ont. M9C 1B2
416-622-4602.

YOUNG ENTREPRENEURS ORGANIZATION (YEO)

Once you've set up a successful business this group can help you navigate through the new challenges you'll experience. The YEO is a volunteer group of business professionals, all of whom are under 40 years of age and who own companies with annual sales of $1,000,000 or more. Their mission is to "Support, educate and encourage entrepreneurs to succeed in building companies and themselves." Check them out at HTTP://WWW.YEO.ORG

10 LOW COST Ways to Promote Your Business

1 **Poster the town:** Place flyers in the following locations; schools, religious centers, malls, community centers, local stores, community bulletin boards, door to door, car windshields (seek permission first).

2 Place an ad in the local newspaper or in specialty newsletters (seniors, chamber of commerce etc).

3 Press releases and articles about your new business in local newspaper.

4 Write an article for local newspapers that showcase your knowledge and skills.

5 Local radio station interviews.

6 Create a web-site or place a banner ad on a local web-site with high traffic for your ideal market.

7 Signage, lawn folding sign for yard work, (obey local signage regulations).

8 Increase traffic with movement, balloons, color, and people greeting or waving at passers-by.

9 The power of references and testimonials. Often people won't take you on your word if you or your business is unknown. Get reference letters or testimonial quotes from someone who can vouch for your abilities and character. The best kind is from a satisfied customer.

10 Use visuals (color, type face and size) to create a logo that can be attached or rubber-stamped onto anything, (bags, t-shirts, ball caps, cars, bikes.) The point is to look professional. Image is very important in promotion of your business

Tips on setting fees and prices

* Research & determine what is fair market value.

* Take minimum wage and multiply by 2.

* Calculate total cost to produce + time to produce, multiply X 2.

* Take a percentage of the deal as a commission.

Multiple Sources of Income (MSIs)

ONCE YOU'VE STARTED and established your business you may find that you have some free time. Many entrepreneurs enjoy the time off as a reward for their hard work. Others seize the opportunity to further increase their wealth. One of the great things about starting your own business is that you invariably uncover other opportunities along the way. And, because you already have the experience and learning from your first company, it's often much easier to set up the second. You already have the knowledge and experience. You also have a track record and perhaps a credit history which will make financing easier. When you enjoy doing what you're doing and you're successful, you'll find that other people come to you with their ideas.

FOR A LOT of entrepreneurs the real fun is in creating and developing businesses. Once it is set up it becomes a management role. Some people lack interest in this area, so it's smart to pass the day-to-day administrative duties to someone who enjoys that job. Meanwhile you get to exercise your creative juices with a new challenge.

> "No matter what I say, what I believe, and what I do, I am bankrupt without love."
> — I Corinthians 13:3

With each additional business you:

1 Create additional streams of income.

2 Reduce your risk, because one business may go out of fashion but you aren't out of business; you just put more energy into the ones that are still working the best.

3 Share resources or exploit underused capacity. For example, you already have a computer or other types of equipment or facilities. You can increase their usefulness.

4 Learn more by expanding your experience base, your list of contacts etc. Even if you eventually decide to take a traditional job sometime in the future your experience will make you more marketable to an employer.

Photo courtesy of Rap-up.com

DEVIN LAZERINE & MISSY ELLIOT

HERE'S AN EXAMPLE of someone who understands the benefits and fun of growing businesses:

> *"You miss 100% of the shots you never take."*
> — Wayne Gretsky
> Hockey Superstar

Success Is All Rapped-Up

Devin Lazerine of Calabases, California first started to experiment with owning his own business when, at age 13, he created a web site that sold ads and various merchandise. Two years later he combined his love of music with an interest in the Internet and launched two successful business-

es: Rap-Up.com, and Rap-Up Magazine.

DEVIN BELIEVES "TEENS can accomplish anything that an adult can if they remain focused and persistent in achieving their goals!" Devin

> **He combined his love of music with an interest in the internet.**

is proof that persistence pays, with current circulation of his magazine exceeding 200,000 and growing! Not only has Devin created a successful business from his hobbies but the industry takes him seriously as well. He has interviewed top hip-hop artists like Craig David, Nelly, Ludacris, 112, Fat Joe and Destiny's Child. He also gets writers from Rolling Stone, The Source, and Vibe to contribute to his magazine.

DEVIN'S ROLE MODELS are Clive Davis, P. Diddy and Russell Simmons, whom he admires for their ability to create multiple businesses with a hip-hop connection. **"My ultimate goal," says Devin, "is to expand my business to include a production company, recording label, clothing line as well as additional magazines."**

WE HOPE YOU'VE been inspired by these great stories and have concluded that the teen entrepreneurs are no different than you and that the only thing holding you back at this point is you. It's about seeing opportunity and then tapping into your creativity to take advantage.

AT THIS POINT we hope you've understood that there are 2 very good ways of making money. One is to budget and invest, the other is to start your own business on either a part or full time basis. They are equally valid. Don't feel bad if you're not comfortable with the entrepreneurial life. Please set your own goals. Always consult people with more experience, but don't ever let anyone dissuade you from reaching for your dreams.

Chapter **Summary** List

1 What entrepreneurial insights did you learn about yourself after doing the assessments in this chapter?

_____

_____

2 Which business idea excites you the most? Why?

_____

_____

3 What do you think will be the biggest challenges facing you with your idea? How will you overcome them?

_____

_____

4 What possible additional streams of income could be spun off from your original idea?

_____

_____

5 What is your next step?

_____

_____

6 What additional resources or assistance do you need to help you get to the next stage?

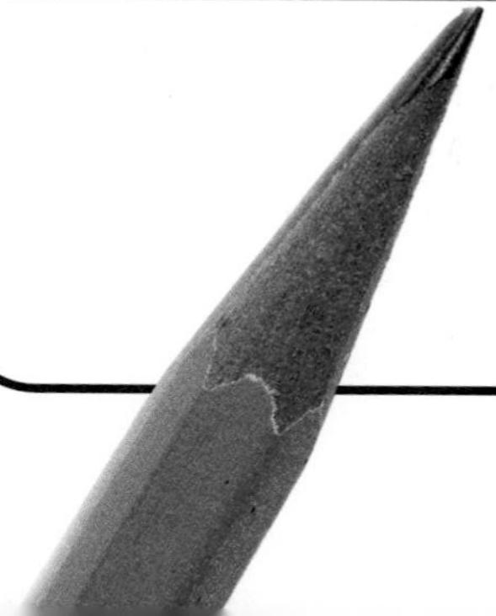

_____

_____

IF YOU HAVE little interest in money-making we hope that you still got something of value from reading this book and doing the exercises. Many of the principles we are trying to share are valid whether you're trying to make a lot of money or any other goal— higher marks or winning the championship with your school team. In short we hope this book becomes the edge you need to get what you want and, most importantly, to want what you get. There are more resources and information available on our web-sites **WWW.ABCS4TEENS.COM** and www.abcsofmakingmoney.com We are also interested in hearing about your success stories. We will share the best ones on our websites and in future books.

> "The future belongs to those who believe in the beauty of their dreams."
> — Eleanor Roosevelt

THIS BOOK

Throughout our experience and our research for this book we have seen thousands of examples of teenagers accomplishing amazing things. You have been an inspiration to us and to return the favor we are dedicating a portion of all retail book sale profits from this book to various children's charities. We hope that in some small way we can be part of your success story.

GOOD LUCK